Celebrate each day!
Christy Rost

CELEBRATING
Home

A Handbook
for Gracious Living

Christy Rost

Photography by Rick Souders

bright sky press
HOUSTON, TEXAS

bright sky press
HOUSTON, TEXAS

2365 Rice Blvd., Suite 202
Houston, Texas 77005

Library of Congress Cataloging-in-Publication Data on file with publisher.

10   9   8   7   6   5   4   3   2   1

Photography, Rick Souders
Editorial Direction, Lucy Herring Chambers
Creative Direction, Ellen Peeples Cregan
Design, Marla Garcia

Printed in Canada through Friesens

TO MY HUSBAND RANDY,

MY HERO, WHO KEEPS OUR WORLD TURNING

EACH TIME I WRITE ANOTHER BOOK

TABLE
of CONTENTS

ACKNOWLEDGMENTS

Writing a book is rarely the work of one person, and in the case of *Celebrating Home*, there are many who have helped me create this beautiful volume. I'd like to take this opportunity to say a heartfelt thank you to these very special friends.

To Lucy Chambers, Ellen Cregan, Kathleen Sullivan, Marla Garcia, Laura Sheinkopf, and the other talented professionals at Bright Sky Press who fell in love with my vision for this book. Who would have guessed their office is located within walking distance of Randy's and my first house. As Lucy said to me shortly after we agreed to publish this book together, "It's a sign!" And to Kathleen Hughes, who suggested Bright Sky Press in the first place!

My sincere thanks to my good friend, culinary colleague, and very talented photographer, Rick Souders and his gifted team at Souders Studios in Golden, CO—John Wood, photographer and Square Pixels retouching and digital imaging, Robin Reed, photographer and Souders Studios manager, and Shelly Ruybalid, food stylist. Years ago, Rick told me he would like to shoot the photos for one of my books. It was pure delight watching your inspired approach at *Swan's Nest* as you and your team transformed my recipes and the mountain home in which Randy and I live into visual magic.

Special thanks to Robert Schueller and my friends at Melissa's Produce in Los Angeles, CA, who provided much of the gorgeous, fresh produce for my recipes, and to Sherie Sobke at Alpine Earth Center in Silverthorne, CO who helped select and repot plants for my basket arrangements. I couldn't have done it without all of you!

My heartfelt gratitude to my dear friend Mario Rinaldi, exclusive USA representative of Champagne Paul Goerg and Simone Johnson for their contribution of exquisite magnums of Champagne Paul Goerg 1er Cru during a *Celebrating Home* pre-publication reception in New York City. And to Chef and owner Charlie Palmer, Yulia Florinksaya, and the excellent, friendly staff at Aureole Restaurant on 42nd Street in New York for your warm and generous hospitality in hosting the reception. It was a glorious evening I'll always remember.

A special thank you to the many companies and individuals who had a hand in creating my *Swan's Nest* studio kitchen, where many of the recipes were developed and photographed: Brian Maynard, Deborah O'Connor and Beth Robinson, of KitchenAid/Whirlpool; Justin Newby of Digitas; Max Caldas, Connie Edwards, Linda McLaughlin, and Lee Schutter of American Woodmark Corporation and Waypoint Living Spaces cabinetry; Zodiaq by DuPont quartz countertops; J.D. Bidwell of J.D. Bidwell Furniture and Trimworks in Denver, CO; Belle and Bob Walstad of Tops in Stone in Colorado Springs, CO; Bill Tinker of All-Electric, Sharon Bellina of Bellina Painting, and Brandon Benson of Appliance Pro in Breckenridge, CO; and Phil and Kelly Stevens of Colorado Custom Wood Floors in Frisco, CO. Your inspired teamwork helped me create the studio kitchen of my dreams!

Behind every large project, there is always someone who is ready to lend a helping hand, inspiration, and encouragement—and in the case of a cookbook, all that recipe tasting! My loving thanks to my dear husband Randy, who contributed recipe ideas, helped the photographers during the photo shoot, washed a million dishes, cooked meals while I wrote the manuscript, and showed his love and support in many ways. Thank you, sweetheart for celebrating each day with me.

And finally, I wish to thank Fran Gallagher, my friend and publicist—a fount of endless enthusiasm, limitless connections, and out-of-the-box ideas. Thank you, dear friend for helping me to achieve this dream.

INTRODUCTION

HOME. *It's the place we return* at the end of the day or after being away for an extended time. It's a tiny urban apartment, a converted loft, a penthouse overlooking the city, a two-story Colonial in the suburbs, a home in the country that's been handed down through the family, a farmhouse in America's heartland, a log cabin tucked in the woods, a beach house just a short walk from the shore, or a rambling ranch house miles from town. It's where we feel safe and secure, refresh our body, renew our soul, love our sweetheart, nurture and love our children, welcome friends, and celebrate the significant and everyday moments in our lives.

Our homes should bring us joy each day. Every home—regardless of whether it's a one-room studio, condo, large apartment, small clapboard house, or mansion—has the capacity to become a warm, gracious, and welcoming place—one that makes us smile as we walk through its rooms. It may be the colors on the walls, heirloom furniture that gleams with a rich patina, a comfy old sofa with bright pillows, windows that frame a beautiful view, a collection of meaningful photographs displayed where we can enjoy them everyday, the sound system splurged on to surround us with music, the way natural light brightens a room, a kitchen that boasts a place for every culinary tool, a graceful staircase, or a tranquil bedroom that feels like a dream each time we climb into bed.

When we take the time to notice and appreciate them, these and other decorative features become small gifts we give ourselves and those who share our lives, and they can provide a reason to smile and celebrate the joy of simply being home.

Through the years, it's always been the little things in our homes that have brought me the most enjoyment. Our first home, a tiny brick house near downtown Houston, was

in desperate need of love and a major overhaul when we purchased it. The built-in corner cabinets in the breakfast nook captured my heart and helped me see past the deplorable condition of the house and envision its possibilities. In our 4th *etage* flat in Paris, where Randy and I lived for a year with our small sons Timothy and Bob, the intricate paneling on the walls, carved marble fireplace, and authentic French doors in each room brought me joy and wonderment that we were actually living in Paris!

Back in the States, our new west-Houston home had the loveliest staircase that made me feel like a queen each time I saw it. After moving to Dallas, where Randy and I still live much of the year, I discovered the beautiful wood paneling in the living room provides a sense of warmth and coziness in winter and refreshing coolness in the middle of hot Texas summers. Our small kitchen, with its floor-to-ceiling bay window overlooking the front yard, provides the perfect spot to observe squirrels racing around the 150 year-old red oak tree, or children riding past on their

bikes, usually with a detour through our circular driveway.

And then there is *Swan's Nest,* our historic home in Breckenridge, Colorado, built in 1898 by a gold baron as a wedding gift for his bride and lovingly restored by us over a period of three years to its former beauty and graciousness. I am awed every day by the breathtaking view of the mountains through our front windows and celebrate that after thirty years of dreaming and planning, Randy and I are truly living a portion of each year in our beloved mountains.

But it's not just the view from *Swan's Nest* that makes me happy. I love the diminutive cherry secretary that's nestled next to the hearth in the living room. I found it in a consignment store in Dallas. It's not an expensive piece, but there's a small crystal lamp resting on it that provides soft light in the evening, and gently illuminates an otherwise dark space with a cheerful glow. It makes me smile each time I pass by, in small celebration of my fortunate "find" and the simple beauty and warmth it provides.

And there's the sunshine that streams through the dining room windows in the mid-morning. It fills the room with light and makes the dining table gleam and the crystal chandelier sparkle like hundreds of diamonds. I can't help but smile as I remember how dark the room was with heavy drapes and light-absorbing wallpaper before we restored *Swan's Nest*.

But, celebrating home is more than the walls, accessories, and history that surround me, more than the view from our windows. It's also the everyday meals Randy and I share at the table, welcome-home dinners when our sons and daughter-in-law Erin come for a visit, time spent with my flowers in the garden, casual summer and early fall gatherings we host for friends on the front veranda at *Swan's Nest*, our annual margaritas-on-the-driveway party for our Dallas neighbors, and festive cocktail parties and cozy meals in winter for our Breckenridge friends.

I've always loved entertaining, from planning the menu and shopping for the freshest ingredients, to setting a beautiful table, creating a centerpiece, and adding gracious touches that pamper and spoil our guests. I'm one of four daughters, and our parents entertained frequently while I was growing up. My sisters and I became the "kitchen crew," so our mother taught us how to set a pretty table, greet and serve guests, assist with the menu, and arrange plates and platters. It was valuable training for me, and it ignited a lifelong passion for entertaining guests in our home and sharing my experience and passion with others through my newspaper columns, television shows, personal appearances, and cookbooks.

I've divided *Celebrating Home* into three sections: Celebrating with Family, Celebrating with Friends, and Celebrating Special Occasions. In each section, I share delectable recipes guaranteed to wow your family and guests, money-saving ideas to create beautiful table settings, practical suggestions to achieve calm and nurturing interiors, helpful guidelines to plan memorable celebrations, and inspiring photographs to assist you in bringing graciousness, beauty, joy, and tranquility into your home.

Because I split my time between two locations—Dallas, Texas, just 400 feet above sea level and Breckenridge, Colorado, at an altitude of 9,300 feet—I've experienced how recipes I have used for years sometimes yield very different results when we're in the mountains. I have therefore written high altitude notes where they will be helpful. If you live in the mountains or spend time there on vacation, *Celebrating Home* can be a resource for recipes that turn out beautifully no matter where you are.

My goal is to inspire you to view your home in a new and fresh way that opens your eyes to the beauty surrounding you each day and gives you reason to celebrate. It is also my goal to empower you with the knowledge and tools you need to accessorize your home in a pleasurable manner, mix and match your tableware and glassware in a creative fashion, develop an eye for using containers in unexpected ways, create floral centerpieces and plant baskets, find joy in preparing meals and enjoying them with family and friends, garnish plates and platters to showcase menus to their best advantage, and master the art of entertaining guests with confidence and style.

Please be my guest and celebrate with me as I invite you into our home, *Swan's Nest*.

> " *My goal is to inspire you to view your home in a new and fresh way that opens your eyes to the beauty surrounding you each day, and gives you reason to celebrate.* "

CELEBRATING
with FAMILY

Consider all the special moments in the life of a family: the first apartment or home, the arrival of a child, birthdays, anniversaries, the annual first day of school, a new job or promotion, graduations, college acceptances, engagements, weddings—the list is endless. Then think about all the days in between: the ordinary days when nothing of particular note occurs, and yet these, too can become reasons to celebrate and embrace life's simple joy. In doing so, we have the opportunity to live our lives at a higher level—one filled with a greater awareness of nature, the gift of family and friends, and the happiness our homes can offer us.

Throughout the years, I've embraced all these moments and many more, transforming them into reasons to celebrate with Randy and our sons. In essence, it's been a way of sharing my passion for entertaining with my family, but on a simpler, everyday scale. The result has been years filled with family meals made memorable by handmade decorations the children brought home from school, seasonal placemats and napkins, colorful glassware and plates to add zest to our everyday table settings, centerpieces created from seasonal materials or mementos collected during vacations, and anything I could imagine that would transform an ordinary meal into a fun-filled gathering.

Sometimes, all it takes to put a refreshing twist on a weekday meal is taking advantage of a sunny, warm day to move the meal outdoors. This unexpected change of scenery somehow makes food taste better, and it can often lead to family members lingering around the table because no one wants to burst the magical bubble created by an impromptu picnic.

When Randy and I are at *Swan's Nest* during the summer we dine outdoors as often as possible. We move a round, wooden table onto our front veranda as soon as the temperatures warm enough for us to be outdoors, and we revel in the opportunity to enjoy dinners while gazing at the mountains. As autumn approaches and the evenings grow chilly, we bundle up, turn on porch lights, and add more candles to the table so we can enjoy every possible moment outdoors.

No matter the season or place you call home, it's possible to add variety to everyday meals by altering where the meal is served. An apartment balcony or condo patio can be outfitted with a couple of chairs and a café table to facilitate al fresco dining during nice weather. But keep in mind that even in the absence of an outdoor spot, or when the weather precludes outdoor meals, nearly every home offers dining options. A coffee table becomes an exotic dining spot with the addition of thick floor pillows, a colorful table runner, favorite music playing in the background, and candlelight. A small table moved in front of the hearth, near a window overlooking the garden, or by a staircase in the entry can transform an everyday mealtime into a resort-like experience.

Rotating various sets of dishes, glassware, tablecloths, placemats, napkins, and centerpieces according to the season or holiday—even a minor one—is another easy and energizing way to transform an ordinary day into an anticipated occasion. I'm always on the lookout for colorful dishes and glassware I can add to my collection to freshen up our table settings. Outlet stores are a great source, but so are garage and estate sales, flea markets, and consignment stores. I also shop department stores regularly, as they typically place seasonal merchandise on sale just before the change of season.

Celebrating family extends far beyond meals enjoyed around the table. Homes nurtured with love and care, and accessorized with an eye toward comfort, graciousness, and the creation of cherished family memories can inspire a celebratory spirit in all who live there. The process begins by identifying a home's attributes and accessorizing them so they may be enjoyed by simply walking through a room. A bay window, pretty staircase, arched doorways, carved doors, window seats, high ceilings, dreamy kitchen, and a host of limitless characteristics provide a foundation on which to decorate your home so it brings a smile to your face each day.

Within these pages, I'll share ideas to help you see your home in fresh, new ways; then provide money-saving decorating tips to help you achieve the look and feel you desire. I hope to inspire you to slow down and enjoy the simple pleasures your home can deliver, for we have the power to influence our families with our positive attitude and the simple joys we embrace every day. When you take the time to appreciate the way the sun streams in a window and casts a glow in your favorite room, your momentary pleasure translates to your family through your smile.

You'll also find recipes I've developed to add spice to family meals. Comfort dishes like manicotti and beef barley soup are presented along with an elegant tilapia with lemon-butter wine sauce and Tex-Mex favorites such as grilled chicken with tomatillo salsa verde and black beans. And I haven't forgotten backyard family picnics! You'll discover scrumptious recipes for grilled butterflied turkey, picnic potato salad, cherry rhubarb tart, and so much more. A renewed enjoyment of your home and family is just moments away.

"I'm always on the lookout for colorful dishes and glassware I can add to my collection to freshen up our table settings."

Sesame Chicken Satays

I'm always seeking ways to bring families together around the table for a meal. These are the moments that create lifetime memories, build communication between parents and their children, and keep everyone connected. Adding an unexpected dish everyone can pick up and eat with their hands is definitely a way to bring people to the table. Think how much fun it is to eat pizza. It's not just the flavor and texture that makes it a family favorite. It's the fact that we can pick it up with our hands—a guarantee of smiles and animated conversation.

For a family meal that's satisfying and fun, this tasty chicken-on-a-stick delivers! The family will come running when the aroma of these sweet and savory satays wafts through the house, and when they see it's dinner-on-a-stick, they'll be putty in your hands. Best of all, the satays cook in minutes! YIELDS 6 SERVINGS

INGREDIENTS

3	large boneless, skinless chicken breasts
½	teaspoon onion powder
	Kosher salt and freshly ground black pepper, to taste
½	cup honey
1	tablespoon soy sauce
2	tablespoons sesame seeds
15	12-inch wooden skewers
1	tablespoon olive oil

Slice each chicken breast into 5 long strips, about ¾-inch thickness. Thread the meat onto wooden skewers and lightly season with salt, pepper, and onion powder. Preheat a grill pan or griddle over medium heat, add the oil, and swirl to coat the bottom of the pan. Cook the chicken skewers 3 to 4 minutes on each side or until the meat is done.

Pour the honey into a dinner-size plate and stir in soy sauce and a dash of salt. Dip the meat into the honey mixture, sprinkle it with sesame seeds, and cook 30 seconds more on each side to sear the glaze. Transfer the satays to a platter and serve.

Grilled Honey-Lime Chicken

Here's something different for backyard grill parties—sweet and tangy grilled chicken breasts that transition easily from casual cookouts to a Tex-Mex fiesta. The flavor secret starts with freshly squeezed lime juice, a bit of lime zest, and locally-produced honey. The chicken absorbs the sweet, citrusy flavors in half the marinade before grilling, and the rest is mopped onto the chicken during the final minutes of cooking, which produces a beautiful, dark glaze. YIELDS 4 TO 6 SERVINGS

INGREDIENTS

4-6	boneless, skinless chicken breasts
½	cup honey, preferably locally-produced
1	tablespoon freshly squeezed lime juice
1½	teaspoons lime zest
¼	teaspoon Kosher salt
¼	teaspoon freshly ground black pepper
1	lime, rinsed and sliced, for garnish

In a small bowl, stir together the honey, lime juice, lime zest, salt, and pepper. Place the chicken in a large plastic zipper bag, pour in half the marinade, reserving the rest, seal the bag, and marinate the chicken in the mixture 1 hour or all day, turning the bag over several times to keep the meat well-coated.

Preheat the grill and reduce the heat to medium-low. Lightly pat the chicken dry with paper towel and place it on the grill, smooth side down. Cook 4 to 5 minutes, turn it over, and cook 4 to 5 minutes more. Rotate and turn the meat over again, baste it well with some of the reserved marinade, and cook 2 to 3 minutes. Turn it over, baste with marinade, and cook 1 to 2 minutes, or until the chicken is done and a meat thermometer registers 165 degrees. Place the meat on a platter and garnish with slices of lime.

Everyone's Favorite Chicken and Rice

Embrace the day and celebrate the simple joy of comfort food. We all experience times when nothing satisfies quite as well as pure comfort food, whether it's a cold winter day, a week when we're not feeling our best, or a time when we just want to share a little savory "lovin-from-the-oven" with our kids. This chicken and rice casserole is nothing fancy—just sheer comfort-in-a-dish. It features simple ingredients found in most kitchens—rice, chicken breasts, onion, celery, and dried herbs. Best of all, this is a one-dish meal. Now that's something to celebrate! YIELDS 4 SERVINGS

INGREDIENTS

1   cup long grain rice
¼   teaspoon curry powder or cumin
¼   teaspoon coarse salt
¼   teaspoon dried basil
½   cup onion, peeled and diced
½   cup celery, rinsed and diced
1¾   cups chicken broth
3   boneless, skinless chicken breast halves
       Coarse salt and freshly ground black pepper,
       to taste
1   tablespoon chopped fresh parsley or cilantro

Preheat the oven to 375 degrees. Pour the rice into a large, heat-proof casserole dish and top with onion and celery. In a small bowl, stir together the curry powder, ¼ teaspoon of salt, and basil, and sprinkle the mixture over the vegetables and rice.

Season the chicken on both sides with salt and pepper and place it on top of the vegetables. Pour the chicken broth over the chicken, cover, and bake 45 to 50 minutes, or until the chicken is done and the rice has absorbed all of the liquid. Garnish with chopped parsley and serve.

Grilled Southwest Chicken Breasts with Cilantro Pesto

When I arrived in Texas as a college student, I had never tasted cilantro and had no idea what Tex-Mex was. I'll admit, for my Midwest and New England palate, it wasn't love at first bite, but now I crave the spicy Southwest cuisine and back-of-the-throat "kick" that's so much a part of the culture surrounding me.

Whether Randy and I are in Texas or Colorado, cilantro often finds its way into every-day dishes and gatherings with friends. This cilantro pesto is a versatile, mouth-tingling change from the usual sweet basil version. I like to serve it as an accompaniment to grilled fish, sautéed chicken breasts, or enchiladas. YIELDS 6 TO 8 SERVINGS

INGREDIENTS

- 2 cups fresh cilantro, rinsed, dried, and coarsely chopped
- ¼ cup pine nuts
- 1 tablespoon jalapeño, seeded and chopped
- 1 tablespoon freshly squeezed lime juice
- 1 tablespoon red wine vinegar
- ¼ teaspoon Kosher salt
  Freshly ground black pepper, to taste
- ¼ cup olive oil
- 6-8 boneless, skinless chicken breasts, rinsed and dried on paper towels
  Kosher salt and freshly ground black pepper, to taste
- 1 teaspoon cumin

In the bowl of a food processor, combine the cilantro, pine nuts, jalapeño, lime juice, vinegar, salt, and pepper. Cover and pulse several times just until the ingredients are mixed. With the processor running, add the oil in a slow stream, until the oil is incorporated and the pesto has a slightly coarse texture.

Preheat the grill. Place the chicken breasts on a cutting board between 2 sheets of plastic wrap and pound them to ¾-inch thickness with a meat mallet or the bottom of a cast iron skillet. Season them with salt, pepper, and cumin. When the grill is hot, place the meat on the grill, smooth side down, cook 4 minutes, and turn them over. Cook 4 minutes more, rotate and turn them over, and cook 2 minutes on each side or until a meat thermometer registers 165 degrees.

Transfer the chicken to dinner plates, garnish with cilantro pesto, and serve with black beans, tortilla chips, and tomatillo salsa verde.

Black Beans

I serve black beans frequently for their nutritional value, great flavor, and versatility. It's so easy to open a can of black beans and spoon them on salads, inside a chicken wrap, or simply mix them with chopped onion, bell pepper, cilantro, freshly squeezed lime juice, and a little coarse salt and pepper to serve as a summertime salad or dip for chips.

When I want to enjoy black beans as a side to Tex-Mex fare, I prefer the flavor and texture I can only get by starting with uncooked beans. In this recipe, the beans soak for a mere two hours before cooking—a great time saver. But if I'm making this recipe in the mountains, I soak the beans overnight, as dry beans take a long time to cook at high altitude unless they are sufficiently presoaked.

I love these black beans as an accompaniment to grilled lime chicken, enchiladas, or just about anything Tex-Mex. They're spicy and full of flavor, with just a touch of heat from the jalapeño and cayenne pepper. I've incorporated bacon for added flavor, but if you prefer a vegetarian version, replace the bacon with two tablespoons of canola oil. With a simple garnish of chopped onion and bright red bell pepper, you'll find these beans add a pop of color to so many menus. YIELDS 8 TO 10 SERVINGS

INGREDIENTS

1	16-ounce package dry black beans
3	strips bacon, diced
1	large sweet onion, finely chopped
1	large jalapeño pepper, stemmed, seeded and diced
5	large cloves garlic, peeled and minced
2	teaspoons cumin
1	teaspoon cayenne pepper
3	cups chicken broth
1	cup water
1	teaspoon salt
2	tablespoons finely chopped onion, for garnish
2	tablespoons finely chopped red bell pepper, for garnish

Pour the beans into a large bowl, pick through them to remove any stones, and rinse well with water. Add enough water to cover, soak the beans 2 hours, then drain.

In a large pot over medium heat, cook the bacon until it renders its fat. Stir in the onion and jalapeño, and cook 3 to 4 minutes until they have softened. Add the garlic, cumin, and cayenne pepper, and cook 1 minute more, stirring constantly. Add the drained beans, chicken broth, and water, and stir gently.

Bring the mixture to a boil, reduce the heat to low, cover, and simmer 1 ½ hours, or until the beans are tender, stirring occasionally. Raise the heat to medium, set the lid ajar to allow steam to escape, and cook 10 to 15 minutes to reduce the liquid by half, stirring frequently. Remove the beans from the heat and keep them warm. To serve, garnish the beans with chopped onion and red bell pepper.

Tomatillo Salsa Verde

One of my favorite aspects of going out for my Tex-Mex "fix", is the chips and salsa the waiter brings while I'm making my selection from the menu. Warm, slightly salty, crispy tortilla chips, served with green salsa verde always perk up my palate and make my mouth and throat tingle—the perfect accompaniment to a frosty margarita or refreshing glass of iced tea.

If you've always wondered what to do with those light green, tomato-looking things with the thin husk you keep seeing in the produce section of your market, this recipe is an easy, flavorful way to expand your culinary prowess. Simply pull off the husks, slice the tomatillos in half, and roast them in the oven until they are soft. Whirl them in the food processor or blender with a couple of ingredients, and you have the best green salsa.

My version of salsa verde delivers just the right amount of heat. It's versatile and tasty as a sauce for grilled or sautéed chicken or pork, or you can serve it on top of enchiladas, scrambled eggs, in burritos, or with tortilla chips for a Tex-Mex fiesta with family and friends any night of the week! YIELDS 1 ¾ CUPS

INGREDIENTS

1   pound tomatillos, about 8 medium
1   large jalapeño pepper, rinsed, seeded, and chopped
¾   cup sweet onion, chopped
¾   cup fresh cilantro leaves
1   teaspoon cumin
¾   teaspoon coarse salt
     Freshly ground black pepper, to taste
     Juice of ½ lime

Preheat the oven to 400 degrees. Remove the husks from the tomatillos and discard. Rinse and dry the tomatillos on paper towels. Slice them in half, place them on a cookie sheet covered with a piece of parchment paper, and fold up each side of the paper to contain any juices that escape during roasting. Roast 15 to 20 minutes, or until the tomatillos brown lightly on top. Remove them from the oven and set them aside to cool.

Transfer the tomatillos and any juices which have accumulated into a food processor. Add jalapeño, onion, cilantro, cumin, salt, pepper, and lime juice. Cover and process until all the ingredients are mixed and the salsa is slightly thick. Spoon the salsa over a recipe or pour it into a serving bowl and serve immediately. Alternately, the salsa may be covered and chilled up to 1 week.

Here's an easy, no-fuss way to seed and chop a jalapeño or other chili pepper. Slice both ends from the pepper and discard them. Stand the pepper upright on a cutting board and slice downward, avoiding the seeds. Keep turning the pepper and slicing downward until the core of seeds remains, and the slices of pepper are ready to be chopped.

Ginger Chicken and Rapini with Thai Sweet Chili Sauce

Between my junior and senior years of high school, I had an incredible opportunity to be a foreign exchange student to Japan. That summer changed my life. It transformed me from a quiet, shy student into an outgoing, self-confident young woman. After all, I received three marriage proposals that summer! Who wouldn't feel confident?

It also introduced me to a cuisine and culture I knew very little about. I loved the chopsticks my family gave me when I arrived in Tokyo and sent home with me when I returned to the States, the hot, fragrant miso soup my Japanese grandmother served each morning, soba noodles I never quite mastered to slurp like my Japanese mother and sisters, and sushi that came in so many beautiful varieties. I consumed so much sticky rice that summer, I arrived home thirty pounds heavier than when I left.

Whenever I create a stir-fry dish, I am reminded of that summer in Japan and set our table with the precious chopsticks my family presented to me when I arrived in Tokyo. They're perfect for this quick chicken and vegetable stir-fry that sizzles with heat from arbol red chiles, balanced with a pleasant sweetness from the chili sauce. YIELDS 4 SERVINGS

INGREDIENTS

2	boneless, skinless chicken breast halves, cut into 1-inch pieces
2	teaspoons cornstarch
2	tablespoons canola or peanut oil, divided
4	green onions, rinsed and chopped, white and green parts
1	medium sweet onion, peeled and coarsely chopped
5	ribs bok choy, rinsed and chopped, white and green parts
¼	pound snowpeas, rinsed and trimmed
½	pound rapini or broccoli rabe, rinsed and chopped, stems and leaves
1	tablespoon fresh ginger, peeled and finely chopped
2	large cloves garlic, peeled and minced
2	dry arbol chiles
½	cup sweet chili sauce
1½	tablespoon soy sauce
1	tablespoon chicken broth

Preheat a wok or large skillet over medium-high heat. In a medium bowl, toss the chicken with the cornstarch until it is lightly coated. Add 1 tablespoon of the oil to the wok and add the chicken. Cook 3 to 4 minutes, stirring constantly, until the meat is just cooked through. Transfer the meat to a serving bowl and keep it warm.

Pour the remaining oil into the wok and add green onions, sweet onion, and bok choy. Cook 2 minutes, stirring frequently, until the onions are crisp-tender. Add snow-peas and rapini, and cook 2 minutes more until the rapini has wilted. Stir in the ginger and garlic, sauté 30 seconds, and add the arbol chiles, sweet chili sauce, soy sauce, and chicken broth, stirring well to combine. Return the meat to the wok and cook 3 to 4 minutes, stirring frequently, until the vegetables are crisp-tender and the meat is hot.

Serve with steamed or fried rice.

A Seasonal Welcome

Make your home a place of beauty and welcome, starting at the street. Trees flush with early-spring blossoms, a leafy canopy in the summer, vibrant color in the fall, and stately branches in the winter, provide interest and a sense of welcome all year long. Garden beds anchored with a variety of shrubbery, accented with seasonal color, evoke pleasure each time you and your guests arrive.

Each season, I take cues from nature to ensure our front porch reflects the same degree of welcome my family and guests will find within. In the springtime, I mix baskets of spring flowers and bunny rabbit art in every size and form with an old pale-blue, milk-washed wooden wheel barrow placed adjacent to the front door. In the summer, I arrange pots of colorful geraniums, petunias, and ivy along the outside edge of the front steps and in large-formal planters on each side of the front door. Containers bloom profusely with pastel impatiens in the shade of the large veranda, hanging baskets sway in the breeze above the porch railing adding additional color and interest, and a tall and graceful Victorian plant rack, given to me by my friend Angel, overflows with blooms. The overall effect is enchanting, restful to those who linger on the veranda, and creates a warm sense of welcome.

In the autumn, which is rather brief in the mountains, freezes come early, so I bring flowering pots indoors to extend their blooming season. In their place, I arrange bales of straw on the front porch, accented with large pumpkins, squash, Indian corn, baskets of pinecones, and a grinning scarecrow. In the winter, when cold winds blow and snow covers the ground for months, I combine nature and whimsy. Planters that hold blooming plants in the summer are filled with armloads of fragrant pine boughs, Randy's childhood Flexible Flyer makes an appearance along with his ice skates and mine. A cheerful, five foot tall, plush snowman greets all who approach.

For those who live in apartments or condominiums, your front door may not open to the street, but you can still provide a seasonal welcome for guests and for your own enjoyment. A seasonal wreath on the front door is a sign that a warm welcome waits within and provides a festive greeting for guests and neighbors. If your front door is recessed from the hallway, consider placing a small table or narrow bookcase next to your door and accessorize it as you would a similar piece in an entry hall. Books, seasonal accessories, and a small lamp provide a gracious feeling of home in an otherwise communal passage.

" Trees flush with early-spring blossoms, a leafy canopy in the summer, vibrant color in the fall, and stately branches in the winter provide interest and a sense of welcome all year long."

Beef Burgundy

The secret to this classic dish is browning the meat. Many cooks have a tendency to stir too soon, instead of allowing meat to sit on the bottom of the pan to brown. The result is steamed meat without brown drippings loaded with flavor that make a great sauce. For a family meal or a gathering with friends, this slow-cooked, hearty beef stew is fragrant and satisfying on a chilly autumn or winter day. YIELDS 8 SERVINGS

 TIP: It takes longer for meats, most vegetables, and potatoes to cook at high altitudes, so cut the meat into 1-inch cubes and the carrots into 1-inch lengths. Add the potatoes to the stew during the final 35 to 40 minutes of cooking time to ensure they are knife tender.

INGREDIENTS

3½	pounds boneless beef chuck roast, cut into 2-inch cubes
2	tablespoons olive oil, divided
1	large sweet onion, peeled and coarsely chopped
5	carrots, rinsed, peeled, and sliced into 2-inch lengths
6	large cloves garlic, peeled and coarsely chopped
1½	cups dry red wine
¾	cup beef stock or broth
3	sprigs fresh Italian parsley
2	sprigs fresh marjoram
1	sprig fresh thyme
2	celery tops with leaves
2	bay leaves
¾	teaspoon kosher salt
¼	teaspoon freshly ground black pepper
1¾	pounds small red potatoes, about 12 to 14

Preheat a large Dutch oven over medium heat, add 1 tablespoon oil, and enough of the meat to form a single layer in the pot. Brown the meat 2 to 3 minutes without stirring, then turn the meat and brown it on the other side. Transfer it to a large bowl, add the remaining oil to the pot, and cook the remaining meat in batches, transferring it to the bowl as it browns. The meat should still be pink inside.

Add onion and carrots to the Dutch oven and cook 3 minutes, stirring often until they begin to caramelize from the brown bits on the bottom of the pot and the onion begins to soften. Add garlic and cook 1 minute more, stirring often.

Pour in the wine and beef stock, stir to loosen any brown bits remaining on the bottom of the pot, and return the meat to the pot. Tie the sprigs of parsley, marjoram, and thyme together with string and drop the bouquet garni into the pot with the celery tops and bay leaves. Bring the mixture to a boil, reduce the heat to low, and cover. Simmer 1 hour, stirring occasionally. Season the stew with salt and pepper to taste and add the potatoes. Cover and continue simmering until the meat and potatoes are knife tender, about 25 to 30 minutes.

Beef Barley Soup

On a cold winter day, there's nothing quite as comforting as a hot bowl of soup. This hearty version features a rich meaty broth, vegetables, barley, and tender pieces of beef that slowly simmer on the stove with only occasional attention. Add a crisp garden salad and a loaf of warm, crusty bread for the perfect cold-weather casual meal.

YIELDS 8 TO 10 SERVINGS

 TIP: Dense vegetables such as carrots can take a long time to become tender when cooked at high altitude. For this soup, I suggest slicing the carrots no more than ½-inch thick so they'll be fully cooked when the soup is served.

INGREDIENTS

2	tablespoons olive oil, divided
½	pound beef soup bone
3	pounds beef chuck roast, trimmed and cut into 1-inch cubes
1½	cups onion, peeled and chopped
1½	cups carrots, rinsed, peeled, and chopped
1½	cups celery, rinsed and chopped
4	large cloves garlic, peeled and chopped
5	cups beef stock or broth
4	cups water
1	bay leaf
1	bunch fresh celery leaves
¾	teaspoon Kosher salt
	Freshly ground black pepper, to taste
¾	cup barley

Preheat a large Dutch oven over medium heat, add 1 tablespoon of the oil, and swirl to coat the bottom of the pot. Brown the bone in the oil until it is well seared. Transfer the bone to a large bowl and add one-third of the meat to the pot. Cook the meat without stirring until the bottom of the meat is brown, then turn it over and brown the other side. Transfer the meat to the bowl with the bone, add the remaining oil to the pot if needed, and continue browning the remaining meat in small batches, transferring it to the bowl as it browns.

Add onion, carrots, and celery to the pot, and cook 5 minutes, stirring frequently, until they caramelize in the meat juices and begin to soften. Add garlic, stir, and cook 1 minute more. Stir in the beef stock and water, return the meat and bone to the pot, and add the bay leaf and celery leaves. Cover and bring the mixture to a low boil, reduce the heat to low, and simmer 2½ to 3 hours, stirring occasionally, until the meat is tender and a rich, dark broth has formed.

Stir in barley, season the soup with salt and pepper, cover, and simmer over low heat, stirring occasionally, until the barley is plump and tender, about 35 to 40 minutes. Remove the bone, bay leaf, and celery leaves, and serve.

Cast Iron Sirloin Steak with Wild Mushroom Cabernet Reduction

If you love dining in a fine steakhouse and tucking into a thick and juicy, buttery-flavored steak, you'll love this recipe. There's no need to heat the grill. A cast iron skillet does the honors in dramatic fashion, thanks to the addition of clarified butter and a fragrant, robust wild mushroom sauce.

For a casual Texas-style meal, serve the steak with beans, coleslaw, and cornbread, but if you have your heart set on romance, serve an elegant first-course soup or salad and a wild rice medley. Don't forget the candlelight! YIELDS 2 TO 4 SERVINGS

INGREDIENTS

1   1-inch thick boneless sirloin steak, about 1 pound
    Coarse salt and freshly ground black pepper
¼   cup unsalted butter, melted
2   large cloves garlic, peeled and finely chopped
½   cup dry red wine
½   cup beef stock or broth
2   tablespoons unsalted butter
1   cup fresh white mushrooms, sliced
¾   cup fresh oyster mushrooms
¾   cup fresh shitake mushrooms
1   tablespoon Italian parsley, chopped

Melt ¼ cup butter in a small saucepan or in the microwave at 50 percent power. Spoon off the white solids and discard. Set the remaining clarified butter aside.

Season the meat generously on both sides with salt and pepper and preheat a large cast iron skillet over medium heat until it is hot. Add 1 tablespoon of the clarified butter to the skillet and swirl to coat the bottom of the pan. Immediately place the meat in the skillet and cook 2 minutes until it browns. Add 1 to 2 additional teaspoons of clarified butter, turn the meat over, and cook 2 minutes more on each side, for a total of 8 minutes cooking time for medium rare. Check the steaks for the desired degree of doneness.

Transfer the meat to a cutting board and keep it warm. Add garlic to the skillet and sauté 30 seconds until it is fragrant. Deglaze the pan with red wine and beef stock, scraping up brown bits from the bottom of the pan. Add the remaining 2 tablespoons of butter and the mushrooms, and cook several minutes until they have softened and the wine sauce has reduced by half.

Slice the meat at an angle and transfer it to a serving platter. Spoon the mushrooms and sauce around the meat and sprinkle the mushrooms with parsley.

Quinoa with Green Onion and Sultanas

Ancient Incas called quinoa the mother grain, and we now recognize this high-protein, complex grain as a "superfood." Quinoa has a delicate flavor and looks like rice, but the grains are smaller and cook quickly. When combined with a flavorful vegetable stock, green onions, and dried fruit, this grain becomes a tasty side dish for meats or fish. For added variety and a nice chewy, crunchy texture, substitute dried cranberries and chopped pecans for the green onions and sultanas. YIELDS 6 TO 8 SERVINGS

INGREDIENTS

1	tablespoon olive oil
1	green onion, green and white parts, rinsed and chopped
⅓	cup Vidalia or other sweet onion, peeled and finely chopped
¼	cup sultanas (golden raisins)
1	cup quinoa
1	cup vegetable or chicken broth
¼	cup water
	Kosher salt and freshly ground black pepper, to taste

In a small saucepan over medium heat, add olive oil and swirl to coat the bottom of the pan. Add green onion, sweet onion, and sultanas, and cook 3 minutes, until the onions have begun to soften, stirring frequently. Add quinoa and cook 1 minute, stirring constantly.

Pour in the vegetable broth and water, stir, and season with salt and pepper. Bring the mixture to a boil, cover, reduce the heat to low, and cook 12 to 15 minutes, or until all of the liquid has been absorbed.

Fluff the quinoa with a fork and serve.

Treating Yourself Like A Guest

Let's face it—life is pretty fast these days. I can recall many times when I've wished there were a few more hours in the day to accomplish everything I needed to get done. It's easy in the midst of these stresses to neglect myself and overlook my own needs for rest and relaxation, so I've created an afternoon ritual and a gracious location that helps me slow down, catch my breath, and reconnect with my inner self.

I've learned to treat myself as a guest during these precious afternoon moments, and the rewards have been tremendous. It's different for everyone, but for me, reconnecting with a quiet sense of grace renews my spirit, my creativity, and my sense of peace. I heat the kettle, prepare a small tray with a favorite china cup and saucer, linen napkin, teapot, and a cookie or other small bite. When the tea is brewed, I retire to my small secretary desk in *Swan's Nest's* living room, or a favorite sofa near the hearth in Dallas, to write a letter to a friend, read a magazine I've saved, or another chapter of a novel. By the time I've finished my pot of tea, I feel calm, refreshed, and re-charged; ready to put a creative spin on tasks that await me.

"...for me, reconnecting with a quiet sense of grace renews my spirit, my creativity, and my sense of peace."

Sweet Onion Glazed Pork Loin Chops

I've always been a fan of caramelized onions. Years ago, I was a spokesperson for an onion brand, so I know a thing or two about cooking with onions. For five weeks every winter, I would travel around the country loaded with skillets, knives, cutting boards, decorative props, and assorted culinary equipment in my suitcase so I could cook in television stations both large and small. By the time I was on my second week, my suitcase and all my clothes smelled of onions and garlic—not bad when in the kitchen, but a bit much when it followed me into airplanes and hotel rooms. I always smelled as if I'd just cooked dinner, and in many cases, I had—even when it was nine o'clock in the morning.

While I'm no longer greeted as "the onion lady" when I walk into television stations, I haven't lost my enthusiasm for the onion's flavor and versatility. I've created a truly wonderful, sweet and tangy onion glaze using sweet caramelized onions, garlic, apple jelly, a splash of apple cider vinegar to balance the sweetness, and smoky paprika. After a quick whirl in the blender, this glaze is simply divine when paired with pork chops. YIELDS 4 SERVINGS

INGREDIENTS

4	1-inch thick boneless pork loin chops
2	tablespoons oil, divided
1	medium-size sweet onion, peeled, halved, and sliced
2	large cloves garlic, peeled and coarsely chopped
¾	cup apple jelly
1	teaspoon apple cider vinegar
¼	teaspoon sea salt
¼	teaspoon freshly ground black pepper
¼	teaspoon smoked paprika
⅛	teaspoon crushed red pepper flakes

"After a quick whirl in the blender, this glaze is simply divine when paired with pork chops."

Preheat a large skillet over medium-low heat, add 1 tablespoon of the oil, and swirl to coat the bottom of the pan. Add the onions and sauté 5 to 10 minutes until they become golden brown. Add the garlic, sauté 1 minute, then transfer the mixture to a blender. Add jelly, vinegar, salt, pepper, and smoked paprika, cover, and blend until the mixture is thick and somewhat coarse.

Place the pork chops in a large plastic zipper bag, pour in the onion glaze, close the bag, and rotate it to coat the meat. Marinate the meat 30 minutes, shifting the bag several times to keep the meat coated.

Preheat the oven to 350 degrees. Preheat a large skillet over medium heat, add the remaining olive oil, and swirl to coat the bottom of the pan. Remove the meat from the marinade, wipe away the marinade with fingers, and transfer it to the skillet. Sear the meat 3 minutes on each side, then transfer it to a roasting pan and cook it in the oven 25 minutes, or until a meat thermometer registers 145 degrees.

While the meat is in the oven, pour the marinade into a small saucepan, bring it to a boil over medium heat, then reduce the heat to low and simmer for 15 minutes. Spoon the sauce over the meat and serve.

Confetti Rice

This is a quick and easy side dish to serve with chicken, fish, or pork. I like to sauté sweet onion and garlic with the rice before adding the liquid, which gives the rice an added flavor dimension. Shortly before it's done, I add chopped green and red bell pepper to provide color and a bit of crunch. For variation, add sliced green onions, peas, chopped nuts, chopped olives, or whatever is in your crisper drawer. For a vegetarian version, substitute vegetable stock for the chicken stock. YIELDS 4 TO 6 SERVINGS

 TIP: Because water boils at a lower temperature at high altitude, the common 2-to-1 liquid-to-rice ratio produces a gummy texture when cooking rice on the stovetop. For fluffy rice at high altitude, I use 1¾ cups liquid for every 1 cup of uncooked rice. The rice may need to cook an additional 5 to 10 minutes until all the liquid has been absorbed.

INGREDIENTS

1	tablespoon olive oil
⅓	cup sweet onion, peeled and finely chopped
1	large clove garlic, peeled and finely chopped
1	cup long grain rice
2	cups chicken stock or broth
	pinch of kosher salt
¼	cup green bell pepper, rinsed, seeded, and chopped into ¼-inch pieces
¼	cup red bell pepper, rinsed, seeded, and chopped into ¼-inch pieces

Preheat a large saucepan over medium-low heat, add oil, and swirl to coat the bottom of the pan. Add onion and sauté 2 to 3 minutes, stirring frequently, until it is soft. Add garlic and cook 30 seconds, stirring frequently. Add rice and cook 1 minute, stirring constantly. Stir in chicken stock and salt.

Raise the heat to medium-high and bring the rice to a boil. Reduce the heat to low, cover, and cook 12 to 15 minutes until most of the liquid has been absorbed. Stir in peppers, cover, and cook until all of the liquid has been absorbed. Fluff the rice with a fork just before serving.

Grilled Butterflied Turkey

As soon as the calendar turns to November, many of us think of turkey dinners, but turkey can be a delicious change from the usual fare any time of the year. I particularly enjoy it when it's cooked on a charcoal grill—an easy, no-fuss entrée for casual gatherings.

I have my husband, Randy, to thank for this recipe. We had one turkey too many in our *Swan's Nest* freezer, so he defrosted one, cut through the back bone and breast bone, and fanned the meat out on the grill, cooking it over a layer of coals. It was a rainy day in the mountains, so we took turns holding a big umbrella over the grill while the other tended to the turkey. The flavor and aroma of the sizzling, juicy, golden brown meat was intoxicating, and I can hardly wait to cook another! YIELDS 6 TO 8 SERVINGS

INGREDIENTS

1   10-to-12-pound turkey, thawed, rinsed,
     and dried on paper towels
1   tablespoon olive oil
     kosher salt and freshly ground black pepper
2   tablespoons butter, melted

Preheat a charcoal grill. Place the turkey, breast side down, on a cutting board. Cut the turkey in half lengthwise through the back bone, using a heavy-duty chef's knife or cleaver. Spread open the turkey and cut through the underside of the breast bone, without cutting into the breast meat and skin. Fan the turkey out so the meat lies flat. Brush the turkey with olive oil on both sides and season with salt and pepper.

Place the turkey, rib side down, on the grill, cover the grill, and cook the meat slowly, 1½ to 2 hours over medium heat, without turning the meat over. Baste the meat occasionally with melted butter as it cooks.

When the meat is done, transfer it to a cutting board, cover it to keep warm, and let it rest 10 minutes before carving.

The Magic Of Lighting

Lighting can make or break a room. Good reading lamps are essential, but the gentle glow of beautiful lighting that softens our mood and makes us feel wonderful when we enter a room is a gift. Lights that gently illuminate a room and focus attention on artwork, an architectural feature, or an attractive corner of the room create sophisticated elegance and have a profound affect on our feeling of wellbeing.

I've always been passionate about lighting, particularly in winter when the days are so short, because I'm a romantic at heart. As the chilly late-afternoons transition into night, I go about the house switching on small lamps, plugging in tiny white lights entwined among decorative accents atop my china cabinet and bookcases, and adjust the dimmers on recessed lighting and crystal chandeliers so they provide the smallest of glimmers. The effect is soft, romantic, elegant, and comforting—the rooms wrap their arms around me and fill me with peace. It's no wonder I adore winter's long nights.

Achieving this look and overall effect is simple and inexpensive. Begin by taking inventory of the lamps you already have, paying particular attention to unique or unusual examples or lamps handed down through the family. Next, make note of the tables and other surfaces in your home such as buffets, bookcases, bedside tables, dressers, fireplace mantles, and kitchen and bathroom countertops.

Using lamps already in your home, move them from room to room until you find the perfect spot for each. This is best done at twilight when you can gauge the effect the lighting creates. Once you determine areas that could be improved by additional mood lighting, check estate and garage sales, consignment stores, and flea markets for unique lighting solutions with history, patina, and charm. For new, inexpensive lighting, furniture stores, home stores, outlet malls, and

even some fabric and craft stores can be good sources. Sometimes, all that's required is a new lampshade or the addition of a decorative finial to transform an ordinary lamp into an attractive lighting accessory.

But, the lighting that exerts the most positive influence on my mood doesn't come from lamps or chandeliers. It's the cheerful illumination of tiny white lights wrapped along the trunk and in the branches of a ficus tree, or glowing softly from greenery that adorns the top of my china cabinet and bookcases. These tiny lights create an atmosphere of celebration and joy every night of the year. Filled with beautiful lamps, chandeliers, and dimly-glowing recessed lighting, nighttime takes on a wonderful feeling of magic.

> "*Lights that gently illuminate a room and focus attention on artwork, an architectural feature, or an attractive corner of the room, create sophisticated elegance.*"

Tilapia with Lemon-Butter Wine Sauce Served Over a Bed of Fennel and Endive

Oven-baking takes a lot of the guess work out of preparing fish, and clean up is a snap. Butter, wine and a squeeze of fresh lemon juice provide a nice balance of flavor for the fish's naturally sweet juices, which are then spooned over the dish just before serving. I like to serve the fish over a colorful, crisp-tender bed of quickly sautéed spicy fennel and tart red endive. YIELDS 2 SERVINGS

INGREDIENTS

½   pound tilapia fillets, rinsed and dried on paper towels

2   tablespoons unsalted butter

2   tablespoons olive oil, divided use

2   tablespoons dry white wine

1   tablespoon freshly squeezed lemon juice
sea salt and freshly ground black pepper, to taste
dash of paprika, for garnish

1   tablespoon shallot, peeled and finely chopped

1   large clove garlic, peeled and finely chopped

1   small fennel bulb, white part only, halved and thinly sliced

1   red endive, halved lengthwise and thinly sliced

2   lemon slices, for garnish

Preheat the oven to 425 degrees. When the oven is hot, melt the butter in a baking dish, taking care it doesn't burn. Remove it from the oven, add 1 tablespoon olive oil, wine, and lemon juice, and swirl the pan to mix.

Dip the fish into the butter mixture, turn it over and place it in the pan. Season the fish with salt and pepper, and sprinkle it lightly with paprika. Cover and bake 12 to 15 minutes, or until it begins to flake.

During the final 6 minutes of baking, preheat a large skillet over medium heat, add the remaining olive oil, and swirl to coat the bottom of the pan. Add shallot, sauté 1 minute until it is soft, add the garlic, and sauté 30 seconds until it is fragrant. Add fennel and sauté 3 minutes until it is crisp-tender, then stir in red endive and sauté 1 minute. Season the mixture with salt and pepper.

Place a bed of sautéed fennel and endive on two dinner plates and top with a piece of fish. Spoon the wine sauce over the fish, garnish with a slice of lemon, and serve.

Penne with Zucchini and Tomatoes

When summer gardens and farmers markets are overflowing with fresh zucchini and basil, celebrate nature's abundance with this fragrant casserole of penne pasta, zucchini, sweet bell pepper, and mushrooms in a zesty tomato sauce.

To dress up this unpretentious casserole, I spoon the pasta into a collection of individual cast iron au gratin dishes, garnish each with grated cheese, and bake. When they're hot and bubbly, I nestle the au gratin dishes within a folded towel on dinner plates. Having personal cast iron pans of pasta makes dinner much more fun! YIELDS 6 SERVINGS

INGREDIENTS

¾	pound penne pasta, cooked almost al dente, drained, and set aside
1½	tablespoons olive oil
½	cup red onion, peeled and chopped
1	yellow bell pepper, rinsed, seeded, and chopped
2	medium zucchini, rinsed, quartered lengthwise, and cut into ½-inch thick cubes
2	cups white mushrooms, cleaned and sliced
3	large cloves garlic, peeled and chopped
3	tablespoons fresh basil, rinsed and julienned
1	tablespoon fresh oregano, rinsed and chopped
1½	teaspoons dried Italian seasoning
	generous grinding of black pepper
⅓	cup freshly grated Parmigiano-Reggiano, for sauce
½	cup freshly grated Parmigiano-Reggiano, for garnish

Preheat the oven to 350 degrees. After the pasta is cooked, preheat a large skillet over medium heat, add the oil, and swirl to coat the bottom of the pan. Add onion and bell pepper, sauté 3 minutes until the onion is translucent, stir in zucchini and mushrooms, and sauté 3 minutes more. Add garlic and cook 1 minute until it is fragrant.

Stir in diced tomatoes, tomato sauce, basil, oregano, Italian seasoning, and black pepper. Cook the mixture 5 minutes until the vegetables have softened and stir in the cheese. Pour the vegetable mixture over the pasta and toss gently to mix. Spray individual au gratin dishes or a 9-by 13-inch pan with nonstick cooking spray and spoon the pasta mixture into the dishes. Sprinkle with the remaining cheese, cover, and bake 40 to 50 minutes, or until the casserole is hot and bubbly.

Three-Cheese Manicotti

This dish was inspired by a manicotti made for me by public television chef, Chris Fennimore of WQED in Pittsburgh, Pennsylvania. I was flying into Pittsburgh to teach cooking classes, and when Chris heard I was coming to town, he told me he'd cook lunch for me in WQED's kitchen studio so we'd have time to visit before my first class. As I walked into the station, I followed the aromas of freshly-baked bread and garlic right to the "WQED Cooks" studio kitchen, where Chris was just pulling a mouthwatering manicotti out of the oven. There's truly nothing as satisfying as comfort food, made with love, shared by two friends.

This is a vegetarian dish, but cooked Italian sausage would be a tasty addition to the sauce if you prefer a heartier manicotti. I love the convenience of assembling the dish ahead and chilling it until shortly before cooking, and it easily doubles to serve a crowd.

YIELDS 4 SERVINGS

INGREDIENTS

1	tablespoon olive oil
⅓	cup sweet onion, peeled and finely chopped
3	large cloves garlic, peeled and finely chopped
1	28-ounce can organic diced tomatoes
1	tablespoon tomato paste
½	teaspoon sugar
½	teaspoon dried sweet basil
	freshly ground black pepper
2	tablespoons fresh oregano, chopped
2	tablespoons Parmigiano-Reggiano
8	manicotti shells
2	ounces cream Havarti cheese, shredded
6	ounces fresh mozzarella
¾	cup part-skim ricotta

Preheat the oven to 350 degrees. Cook the manicotti shells according to package directions just until they are al dente. Drain and cool slightly. Fill each shell with Havarti, mozzarella, and ricotta. Spoon a small amount of sauce into the bottom of a casserole dish, arrange the filled manicotti on top of the sauce, and pour the remaining sauce over the shells. Cover and bake 45 minutes, or until the sauce is bubbly and the filling is hot. Sprinkle with grated Parmegiano-Reggiano just before serving.

Curried Butternut Squash

This quick, stovetop vegetable dish has a lot going on for such a simple recipe. Brown sugar, dried fruit, and the butternut squash's natural sugars provide sweetness, while curry lends spice. At the same time, there's great texture—the softness of the sautéed squash paired with the chewiness of the golden raisins. All these elements combine to create a delightful dining experience. Serve it with roasted Cornish game hen, pork roast, or turkey. YIELDS 4 SERVINGS

INGREDIENTS

1	2¼-pound butternut squash, peeled, halved, seeded and cut into ½-inch cubes, about 4 cups
1½	tablespoons olive oil
⅓	cup golden raisins
1	tablespoon brown sugar
¾	teaspoon curry powder
	dash of sea salt

Preheat a large nonstick skillet over medium heat. Add oil and swirl to coat the bottom of the pan. Add the cubed squash in a single layer and cook 2 to 3 minutes without stirring until the bottom of the squash is lightly browned. Turn the squash over, add raisins, brown sugar, curry powder, and a dash of salt, and cook the squash 2 to 3 minutes per side until it is knife tender and golden brown on all sides, about 10 minutes total.

"*Brown sugar, dried fruit, and the butternut squash's natural sugars provide sweetness, while curry lends spice... All these elements combine to create a delightful dining experience.*"

Roasted Okra and Heirloom Tomatoes

It's difficult to find a Southern cookbook without a recipe for okra. This tasty seedpod, grown in many of the world's regions, is a mainstay in Southern cuisine—often fried, but also used to thicken soups or slowly simmered with tomatoes, onions and savory spices.

In this recipe, I get to enjoy all the flavor of okra without frying. I combine whole pods with thick wedges of heirloom tomatoes, pop them into a hot oven, and roast everything with a drizzle of olive oil, salt, pepper, and a dash of Cajun seasoning. This recipe is designed for four, but I must confess it was so irresistible, I ate enough roasted okra to seriously compromise a guest's portion, so you may wish to cook extra! YIELDS 4 SERVINGS

INGREDIENTS

1   pound fresh okra, rinsed and dried
2   large heirloom tomatoes, stemmed and cut into thick wedges
3   tablespoons olive oil
    kosher salt and freshly ground black pepper, to taste
1-2   teaspoons Cajun seasoning

Preheat the oven to 425 degrees. Line a large cookie sheet with parchment paper and place the okra in a single layer at one end of the pan. Place the tomato wedges in a single layer at the other end of the pan to prevent their juices from reaching the okra as it roasts. If the cookie sheet is not large enough, use two pans.

Drizzle the okra and tomatoes with olive oil and season them with salt, pepper, and Cajun seasoning. Roast the vegetables in the oven 15 minutes, or until the okra is softened and has browned on the bottom. Serve immediately.

Photo from Christy's Scrapbook

Sautéed Bok Choy and Broccoli Rapini

This is a quick, very flavorful vegetable side dish that's fresh and crisp-tender. It features broccoli rapini, sometimes called broccoli rabe—a cluster of leafy stalks with small, broccoli-like florets. I've started using chopped rapini in stir-fries because it cooks quickly and has great texture and flavor. When combined with bok choy, snow peas, green onions, and garlic, there's so much flavor in the pan, the dish only needs a bit of kosher salt and pepper. Try serving it as an accompaniment to a grilled steak or poached salmon, or spoon the vegetables over rice for an Asian-inspired main dish. YIELDS 6 SERVINGS

INGREDIENTS

1	tablespoon canola or grape seed oil
¼	pound snow peas, rinsed and trimmed
1	bunch broccoli rapini, rinsed and coarsely chopped
1	baby bok choy, rinsed and chopped
2	green onions, rinsed and sliced, white and green parts
2	large cloves garlic, peeled and finely chopped
	kosher salt and freshly ground black pepper, to taste

Preheat a large skillet or wok over medium heat, add oil, and swirl to coat the bottom of the pan. Add snow peas and stir 3 minutes until they begin to soften. Add rapini, bok choy, and green onions, and sauté 4 to 5 minutes until they are crisp-tender. Stir in the garlic and cook 1 minute more. Season the vegetables with salt and pepper, and serve.

Picnic Potato Salad

For summer picnics, backyard barbecues, and casual meals, there's nothing like a chilled bowl of potato salad. To me, the mixture of soft cubes of potato, crunchy bell peppers and onion, and creamy mayonnaise dressing with a hint of spicy mustard signify the arrival of summer's carefree days and ample occasions to celebrate outdoors with family and friends. YIELDS 6 TO 8 SERVINGS

 TIP: Potatoes take longer to cook at high altitude, so when boiling the potatoes, please allow 25 minutes or more for them to become knife tender. Keep an eye on them during the final minutes of cooking, as they can go from not-quite-done to overly soft very quickly.

INGREDIENTS

2   pounds Yukon Gold potatoes, about 6 medium
½   cup green bell pepper, cut into ¼-inch dice
½   cup yellow bell pepper, cut into ¼-inch dice
½   cup sweet onion, peeled and chopped
3   hard-cooked eggs, peeled and chopped
1   cup prepared mayonnaise
3½   teaspoons dry mustard
½   teaspoon kosher salt
     freshly ground black pepper, to taste
4   tablespoons half-and-half
½   teaspoon paprika, for garnish

Place potatoes in a Dutch oven with enough water to cover them, and cook just until they are knife tender, about 15 to 18 minutes. Drain, cool, peel, and cut them into 1-inch cubes. Add bell peppers, onion, and eggs, stir gently, and set the mixture aside.

    In a medium bowl, whisk together the mayonnaise, dry mustard, salt, pepper, and half-and-half until they are well blended. Pour the mixture over the potatoes and toss gently until the potatoes are well coated. Transfer the potato salad to a serving bowl, sprinkle with paprika, cover, and chill until ready to serve.

Daily Rituals

In the late-afternoon, my husband Randy and I step away from our work, pour ourselves a cup of hot tea, a glass of wine or a cocktail, and settle into comfortable chairs flanking the kitchen fireplace for some quiet conversation. It's a ritual we started over thirty years ago when we lived in Paris, one we continue to embrace, especially now that our lives have become increasingly busy. This daily ritual is part of the "glue" that binds us, keeps us close, and provides much-needed relaxation when deadlines loom and the list of to-do's piles up.

Creating an inviting spot for our daily gathering helps make it work. When Randy and I were restoring *Swan's Nest* and designing our kitchen addition, one of the notions we discussed was establishing a spot for sharing a glass of wine and chatting about our day. The location had to take advantage of our gorgeous mountain views, and it needed to be cozy during the long winters when darkness arrives early.

We concluded that a hearth built into a long kitchen wall, adjacent to an expansive bay window would be the focal point for our afternoon gathering. Even before the hearth was fully installed, I knew we had made the right choice. It almost begged to be surrounded by comfy chairs, and I could already picture how serene and inviting the cozy area would be on winter nights or summer afternoons.

In front of the hearth, I placed a unique small octagonal table with a beautiful twisted pedestal I found in a Dallas furniture warehouse. A polished pewter tray rests on the table with a tiny vase of flowers and room for two wine glasses or cups of tea and a plate of cheese. The charming arrangement of chairs and table in front of the hearth invites all who visit to sink into soft cushions and relax. My favorite moments are the quiet times I spend there with Randy.

"It almost begged to be surrounded by comfy chairs, and I could already picture how serene and inviting the cozy area would be on winter nights or summer afternoons."

Cranberry Orange Muffins

Baking at high altitude can be a challenge. Unless the proportions of flour, sugar, leavening, and liquid are adjusted, baked goods rise quickly in the oven only to fall, leaving dashed hopes and a mess to clean up. I've also discovered that flavors often need an added boost at higher altitudes to produce the results I've come to expect in my Dallas kitchen.

I'm happy to say this muffin recipe is one I created in Breckenridge at an altitude of 9,300 feet, and it was a success at first try. Wow! The muffins feature dried cranberries, which I always have in my pantry, so I can whip up a batch at a moment's notice. The big question was what would happen to the muffins' texture when I baked them in my Dallas kitchen? Surprise! They were just as tender and flavorful in Texas with no adjustments to the recipe. No matter where you live, you can bake these delightful muffins with confidence. **YIELDS 2 DOZEN MUFFINS**

INGREDIENTS

½	cup unsalted butter, softened
¾	cup plus 1 tablespoon sugar
1	orange, zested
2	eggs
3	tablespoons freshly squeezed orange juice
3	teaspoons vanilla
3¾	cups flour
2	teaspoons baking powder
¼	teaspoon baking soda
1	teaspoon salt
1¼	cups milk
½	cup dried cranberries
2	tablespoons sugar, for garnish

Preheat the oven to 400 degrees. In the large bowl of an electric mixer, cream butter, sugar, and orange zest until the mixture is light and fluffy, about 5 minutes. Add eggs, beating well after each addition, and stir in the orange juice and vanilla.

In a large bowl, stir together flour, baking powder, baking soda, and salt. Gradually add the flour mixture to the butter mixture, alternately with the milk, to form a thick batter. Stir in the cranberries.

Line muffin tins with paper liners or spray with nonstick cooking spray, and fill them ½ full. Sprinkle the top of the muffins with the remaining sugar and bake 15 to 18 minutes at low altitude, or 18 to 20 minutes at high altitude until they are golden brown and a tester inserted into the center comes out clean.

Chocolate Chip Shortbread Cookies

It's impossible for me to write a book about home without including a recipe for chocolate chip cookies, especially one that bakes beautifully at high altitude. What's a celebration of the first day of school, a letter of college acceptance, or friends dropping by for a visit without a plate of warm-from-the-oven cookies?

I found out the hard way that at high elevations the standard chocolate chip cookie recipe looks pretty in the oven for the first few minutes, only to flatten to the thickness of a sheet of paper—one that needs to be scraped from the cookie sheet directly into the trash. What a disappointment! So began my crusade to develop a chocolate chip cookie that looks pretty, tastes divine, and holds up to baking at any altitude. I think you'll be pleased with this shortbread cookie packed with chocolate chips. YIELDS 3 DOZEN 2½-INCH COOKIES

 TIP: I've baked these cookies in the mountains of Breckenridge and the plains of Dallas with equal success. At high altitude, adjust the oven rack to the upper third of the oven to speed up the baking process. Cookies may take an extra minute or two to brown lightly around the edges.

INGREDIENTS

1¼	cups unsalted butter, softened
½	cup granulated sugar
½	cup confectioners' sugar
2	teaspoons vanilla
2⅓	cups flour
2	tablespoons cornstarch
½	teaspoon baking powder
½	teaspoon salt
1¼	cups semi-sweet chocolate chips

Preheat the oven to 350 degrees and lightly grease cookie sheets. In the large bowl of an electric mixer, cream butter, granulated sugar, confectioners' sugar, and vanilla until the mixture is light and fluffy.

In a medium bowl, stir together flour, cornstarch, baking powder, and salt. Gradually stir the flour mixture into the creamed mixture until it is well blended. Stir in chocolate chips.

Form 1-inch balls of dough with hands, place them 2 inches apart on the cookie sheets, and flatten them to ⅜-inch thickness with the bottom of a glass dipped in flour. Bake 16 to 18 minutes, or until the bottom edges of the cookies begin to brown. Remove them from the oven and transfer them to a wire rack to cool.

Heavenly Sand Tarts

The first time I made these cookies, I shared some with my Breckenridge friend Maggie who accompanies me on the piano Sunday mornings when I cantor. Maggie's husband John loved their buttery-almond flavor and shortbread-like texture, dusted in confectioners' sugar. When Maggie told him the cookies were called Sand Tarts, John replied, "These are too heavenly to be called sand tarts. I'll call them Heavenly Tarts." These cookies gained a new name!

YIELDS 3 DOZEN 3-INCH COOKIES

 TIP: These cookies bake beautifully at high altitude. Adjust the oven rack to the upper third of the oven and increase the baking time to 18 to 20 minutes, or until the top of the cookie feels set when touched lightly with a finger.

INGREDIENTS

1	cup unsalted butter, softened
1	cup confectioners' sugar, sifted
2	cups flour
½	teaspoon salt
2	teaspoons vanilla
1	teaspoon water
1	teaspoon almond extract
⅓	cup toasted sliced almonds, ground
	confectioners' sugar, for garnish

Preheat the oven to 325 degrees. In the large bowl of an electric mixer, cream butter and confectioners' sugar until the mixture is light and fluffy. Add vanilla, almond extract, and water, and beat well.

In a medium bowl, stir together flour and salt, and gradually stir them into the creamed mixture with the ground almonds to form a soft dough. Using lightly floured hands, shape the dough into 1-inch balls, place them on ungreased cookie sheets, and flatten them slightly with the bottom of a glass dipped in flour.

Bake 12 to 15 minutes or until the cookies are set. Dredge them in confectioners' sugar while the cookies are warm, and cool completely on a wire rack. To store, place the cookies in an airtight container with parchment or wax paper between each layer.

Devil's Food Cupcakes with Fudge Frosting

I love the aroma of chocolate "anything" baking in the oven, and these divine chocolate cupcakes with a thick coating of fudge frosting deliver, big-time. The cake is light and tender, not-too-sweet, and has the perfect balance of chocolate flavor. For everyday desserts, after-school snacks, or family birthday celebrations, I love baking a batch of these family-favorite cupcakes. YIELDS 24 CUPCAKES

 TIP: For beautiful devil's food cupcakes at high altitude, substitute 2 cups all-purpose flour for the cake flour, increase the vanilla to 3 teaspoons, and fill each muffin cup ½ full of batter. Adjust the oven rack to the center position, and bake 20-22 minutes.

INGREDIENTS

1	cup milk
2	teaspoons cider vinegar
¾	cup unsalted butter, softened
1½	cups sugar
3	eggs
1¼	teaspoons vanilla
2	cups cake flour, sifted
¾	cup cocoa
1	teaspoon baking soda
1	teaspoon salt
¼	teaspoon baking powder

Preheat the oven to 375 degrees. Stir vinegar into the milk and set it aside to sour.

In the large bowl of an electric mixer, cream butter and sugar until the mixture is light and fluffy, about 8 minutes. Add eggs, one at a time, beating well after each addition. Stir in the vanilla.

In a medium bowl, stir together the cake flour, cocoa, baking soda, salt, and baking powder until they are well blended. Gradually beat the dry ingredients into the creamed mixture, alternately with the sour milk, scraping the bowl often, beginning and ending with the flour mixture. The batter will be thick.

Line muffin tins with paper liners and fill each cup ⅔-full of batter. Bake cupcakes 13 to 15 minutes, or until a cake tester inserted into the center of a cupcake comes out clean. Remove the baking pans from the oven and transfer the cupcakes to a wire rack to cool completely. Do not leave the cupcakes in the baking pans to cool, as they will become soggy. Once cool, frost the cupcakes with Fudge Frosting.

Fudge Frosting

As a topping for devil's food cupcakes, white cakes, or a big pan of brownies, this creamy fudge frosting is thick and decadent with a chocolate flavor you'll love.

YIELDS FROSTING FOR 24 CUPCAKES

INGREDIENTS

2	squares unsweetened chocolate, melted
3	tablespoons unsalted butter, melted
4	cups confectioners' sugar, sifted
	dash of salt
4-5	tablespoons milk
1	teaspoon vanilla
1	tablespoon unsalted butter, softened

In the large bowl of an electric mixer, cream the chocolate, melted butter, confectioners' sugar, and salt alternately with the milk until the frosting is thick and creamy. Add vanilla and soft butter, and beat until they are well blended. Spread the frosting with a knife or offset spatula.

From the time I first started baking in my mother's kitchen, it has been the artistry of baking that inspires me. Simple tools such as offset spatulas, pastry bags, frosting tips, microplanes for zesting citrus fruit and grating chocolate and whole nutmegs, and the pastry wheel pictured here, help me achieve professional results in my home kitchen. I use the pastry wheel to cut long strips of pie pastry with a beautiful fluted edge for the basket weave top crust on my Cherry Rhubarb Tart.

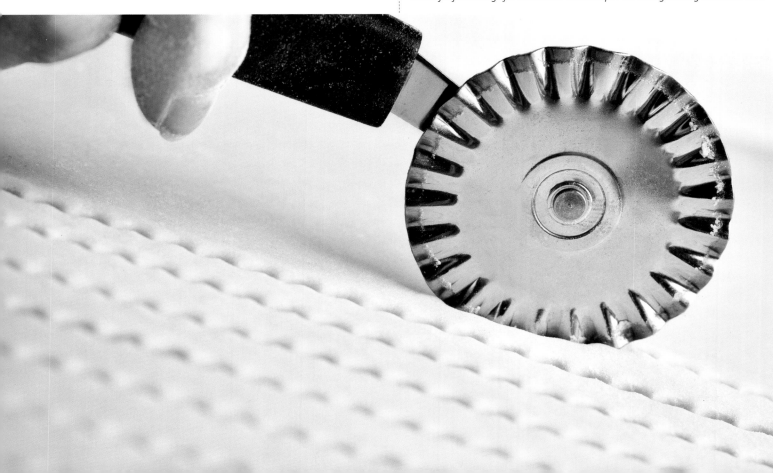

Molasses Spice Cupcakes with Cream Cheese Frosting

A few years ago when I was in the baking aisle of my Dillon, Colorado, supermarket, I overheard a young girl standing in front of the cake mixes ask her mother to bake her a birthday cake. I'll never forget the mother's response. "Cakes don't turn out well at this altitude, honey. Why don't we buy you a cake?" The little girl appeared crestfallen, and it broke my heart.

As a silent pledge to that little girl, I decided my next cookbook would include cake recipes every home chef could bake successfully, whether they live near the ocean or in the mountains. These moist and tender, sugar-and-spice cupcakes, iced with a thick layer of fluffy cream cheese frosting, bake beautifully in both my Texas and Colorado kitchens. They're quick and easy to make for everyday family meals, birthday celebrations, a homemade treat to share with friends and neighbors, or to celebrate the first day of autumn. If you prefer a cake, pour the batter into two 9-inch round pans and bake 25 to 30 minutes. YIELDS 32 CUPCAKES

 TIP: This cupcake recipe needs very little adjustment for high altitude baking. Simply increase the vanilla to two teaspoons, adjust the oven rack to the center position, and bake 20-22 minutes for beautiful results. For a two-layer 9-inch round cake, bake the layers 40-45 minutes.

INGREDIENTS

1	cup unsalted butter, softened
1¾	cups granulated sugar
1	tablespoon light brown sugar, packed
5	eggs, at room temperature
1	tablespoon molasses
1	teaspoon vanilla
3¼	cups flour
1¾	teaspoon baking powder
1	teaspoon salt
1½	teaspoons Saigon cinnamon
1	teaspoon freshly grated nutmeg
½	teaspoon ground cloves
½	teaspoon ground ginger
1	cup buttermilk
⅓	cup milk

Preheat the oven to 350 degrees. In the large bowl of an electric mixer, cream butter, granulated sugar, and brown sugar until the mixture is light and fluffy, about 8 minutes. Add eggs, one at a time, beating well after each addition. Stir in molasses and vanilla.

In a medium bowl, stir together flour, baking powder, salt, cinnamon, nutmeg, cloves, and ginger. Gradually beat the flour mixture, alternately with the buttermilk and milk, into the creamed mixture to create a thick batter.

Line muffin tins with paper liners. Spoon the batter into the tins, filling each cup half full. Bake 18 to 20 minutes, or until a cake tester inserted into the center of a cupcake comes out clean.

Remove the tins from the oven and transfer the cupcakes from the pans to a wire rack while they're still hot so they don't become soggy. Cool completely and frost with Cream Cheese Frosting.

Cream Cheese Frosting

For spice cupcakes and carrot cakes, there's nothing quite as tasty as a generous topping of sweet and tangy cream cheese frosting. This version makes enough frosting for three dozen cupcakes or a two-layer cake. YIELDS FROSTING FOR 3 DOZEN CUPCAKES

INGREDIENTS

6   tablespoons unsalted butter, softened
½   cup (4 ounces) cream cheese, softened
5½   cups confectioners' sugar, sifted
     dash of salt
3-4 tablespoons milk
1   teaspoon vanilla

In the large bowl of an electric mixer, cream butter and cream cheese until they are well blended. Add confectioners' sugar, one cup at a time, alternately with the milk, until the frosting is thick and creamy. Stir in the vanilla.

Photo from Christy's Scrapbook

My mom, Jinx Schnoes, picking rhubarb at Twin Creeks Farm in Freeport, Illinois.

"...there's nothing quite as tasty as a generous topping of sweet and tangy cream cheese frosting."

Cherry Rhubarb Tart

I think of my mom each time I make this tart. My mom grows rhubarb in her Freeport, Illinois, farm garden and generously shares it with her four daughters, going so far as to package and ship it across the country via priority mail. Yes, we can all purchase rhubarb in our local markets, but it's not the same as getting it from Mom. Her rhubarb has thick, sturdy, ruby-red stalks and a sweet-tart flavor.

Last summer when Randy and I visited the farm, Mom took me to her garden to pull rhubarb. Many of the stalks were thigh high, and at one point, I thought I was going to land on my "you-know-what" as I pulled and pulled to release a particularly stubborn stalk from the soil. We broke off the leaves, bundled the rhubarb into paper bags, and carried it back down to the house, where Mom and I cut it into lengths that would fit in my cooler. Then I placed it into plastic zipper bags and chilled it for the trip to Colorado.

When Randy and I reached *Swan's Nest,* I rinsed the rhubarb, cut it into three-quarter -inch lengths, and placed it in freezer bags, reserving some to use immediately. The tart recipe I share with you here is the one I came up with that day. Sweet, yet pleasantly tart, with a woven top crust that glistens with a dusting of clear sparkling sugar, this tart is destined to become a summertime tradition in our home. Maybe in your home, too!

YIELDS 1 10-INCH TART

INGREDIENTS

2	cups flour
3	tablespoons sugar
1	teaspoon salt
¾	cup *cold* unsalted butter, cut into ½-inch cubes
4-5	tablespoons *ice* water
½	teaspoon almond extract
1	21-ounce can cherry pie filling

2	cups fresh rhubarb, cut into ½-inch pieces
⅓	cup sugar
1	egg, for egg wash
1	tablespoon water, for egg wash
1	tablespoon clear sparkling sugar or 2 teaspoons granulated sugar
1	10-inch round tart pan with removable bottom

When making this pastry at high altitude, increase the amount of ice water by 1 to 2 tablespoons to compensate for the dry atmosphere. If the pastry feels dry and cracks easily when rolling it out, add additional ice water, 1 teaspoon at a time, until the pastry is easy to work with. The baking time may need to be increased 5 to 10 minutes, depending on the altitude, so the rhubarb is knife tender.

Place flour, 3 tablespoons sugar, and salt into the bowl of a food processor and pulse several times to mix. Add the butter and pulse until it is pea-size.

Add almond extract and 4 tablespoons ice water, and process at low speed until the pastry is crumbly. If the mixture appears dry, add the remaining ice water and process just until the pastry comes together and forms a ball. Remove the pastry, wrap it in plastic wrap, and chill at least 30 minutes or until it is cold.

In a large mixing bowl, gently stir together the cherry pie filling, rhubarb, and sugar until they are well blended; set it aside.

Preheat the oven to 400 degrees. On a floured pastry cloth or counter, roll the pastry into a 12-inch circle. Fold the pastry in half and transfer it to the tart pan. Unfold the pastry, fit it into the pan, and trim the excess pastry by running a rolling pin over the top of the tart pan. Gather the trimmings together into a ball, roll it out, and cut the pastry into ten ¾-inch wide strips using a pastry wheel or knife. Place 5 strips of pastry across the top of the tart, then turn the tart one-quarter turn and place the remaining pastry strips across the top to form a basket-weave pattern.

In a small bowl, whip the egg and water together with a fork. Brush some of the egg wash over the pastry strips and along the edges of the tart and sprinkle them with sparkling sugar.

Place the tart on a cookie sheet lined with parchment paper and bake 30 to 35 minutes, or until the pastry is golden brown, the filling is bubbly, and the rhubarb is knife tender. Remove the tart from the oven and transfer it to a wire rack to cool.

Creating A Luxurious Bedroom Retreat

I confess, envisioning the décor of our *Swan's Nest* master bedroom took a lot of effort. In fact, during the entire three-year restoration project, I was without a doubt more dumbfounded by how to decorate the master bedroom than any other room in the house. You see, I love a master bedroom that's light and bright, with soft colors that make me feel peaceful and lend a soft, airy atmosphere to the room.

What I was faced with was a large room built over 100 years ago that originally served as the smoking and billiards room, completely paneled in stained wood—even the ceiling! How was I going to transform this spacious, but dark room, with its breathtaking mountain views, into a luxurious, serene bedroom?

Unless we carefully plan and build a house that addresses every need and desire, there are always one or two elements we would change if we could. It's rare to find the perfect house with perfect rooms. The challenge is to approach each room with an open mind and transform perceived negative characteristics into exceptional opportunities to create something divine. A tiny bedroom can then become the cozy room everyone wants, and a lackluster storage room off the kitchen can be transformed into a sewing nook or miniature library for a much-loved cookbook collection.

The day I realized my ideal bedrooms were always "summer" rooms, I was able to step back, change my viewpoint, and approach *Swan's Nest's* master bedroom from an entirely new perspective. I began to regard the space as a "winter" room—a beautiful place where the historic wood walls and ceiling would be an asset instead of a hindrance to creating the luxurious, elegant bedroom I desired.

"...*stroll about your home with a fresh perspective and watch your decorating problems transition into exciting opportunities to create one-of-a-kind rooms you love.*"

Armed with this new perspective, my decorating plans swiftly fell into place. *Swan's Nest* had been the home of Ben Revett, a gold baron born in India of British parents, who together with his wife entertained royalty from Europe, so I embraced that theme and ran with it. The space needed an impressive bed to anchor the room, a comforter and pillows fit for "The Gold Dredge King," oversized bedside tables that reflected European style, a chaise lounge in the bay window to complement our home's Victorian history, a magnificent crystal chandelier Ben Revett would have selected himself, and a light-colored Oriental rug to balance the room's dark tones.

I purchased the heavily-carved, four-poster bed on sale at one of my favorite, family-owned furniture stores in Dallas, and found the bombé chests on a weekend morning at a Dallas estate sale. Lucky for me, a generous estate sale shopper offered to transport them home for me in his pickup truck, as they wouldn't fit in my car! The Italian gold mirrors were a splurge—one of the few items I didn't purchase on sale, but I made up for it by ordering the crystal chandelier online and assembling much of it myself. The gorgeous gold Oriental screen had been in Randy's parents' home and now lends beauty to a corner of our bedroom. And the handmade Oriental rug, with its lovely rose border, was the perfect solution to brighten the entire room.

Using my experience with our master bedroom, stroll about your home with a fresh perspective and watch your decorating problems transition into exciting opportunities to create one-of-a-kind rooms you love. Each time I walk into our *Swan's Nest* master bedroom, I fall in love with it all over again.

CELEBRATING
with FRIENDS

I can organize a gathering of friends at the drop of a hat. Steaks, chicken, or burgers on the grill, a crisp salad overflowing with sliced, fresh vegetables, and a berry tart make summer gatherings effortless and fun. In the fall or winter when I'm craving a savory beef or pork roast and a slice of spice cake, that's all the encouragement I need to pick up the phone and say, "Come for dinner!"

I'm passionate about inviting friends into our home and making them feel welcome. During the nearly three-year restoration of *Swan's Nest*, I didn't allow the lack of electricity or running water to deter me from hosting our new neighbors and friends for summer dinners on the veranda. We hadn't even moved into the house yet, so all my food prep was done in our tiny condo kitchen on the other side of the county. We packed dinner, beverages, ice, glassware, china, silverware, and anything else we needed into coolers and boxes and hauled it over to the house in our car.

I truly believe those relaxed, casual dinners and parties were some of my all-time favorite gatherings. In the midst of a major construction project, guests expected very little and I had a blast exceeding their expectations, in very simple ways. The tablecloths and chairs didn't match, but the magnificent mountain view was hard to beat, the jug of frosty margaritas was always ready, the beer was cold, and we laughed over the lack of home essentials. Some wonderful, lasting friendships were forged over al fresco dinners of grilled chicken or bison steaks, fresh salads—often brought by our guests—corn-on-the-cob, and cherry or peach rustic country tarts.

Even during a particularly cold winter, Randy and I hosted a construction party in *Swan's Nest's* dining room. We still had no heat or running water, but we plugged in several electric heaters and celebrated the electric lights that were installed that very day. There was no furniture in the house, but large cartons containing kitchen cabinets served as a base for sheets of plywood, and a brand new drop cloth made an appropriate table cover. I brought two tall silver candle sticks from the barn for ambiance, lit the candles, and the party was a huge success.

I love an elegant, candlelight gathering, but these examples illustrate how unimportant the surroundings can be when it comes to celebrating with friends. It's the joy of sharing time and simple food together that really counts, and sometimes more fun is had by all when the situation is less than stellar.

Nevertheless, I think it's important to set the stage for guests before they arrive. That can mean anything from arranging lanterns with votive candles along the front walk, to lining the front porch steps with pots of blooming flowers so guests experience a sense of fun and expectation as they stroll to the front door.

"Some wonderful, lasting friendships were forged over al fresco dinners of grilled chicken or bison steaks, fresh salads—often brought by our guests—corn-on-the-cob, and cherry or peach rustic country tarts."

As you explore this section, you'll discover many ideas for inspired home gatherings, with an emphasis on simplicity, creativity, money-saving solutions, and fun. From taking advantage of small spaces in your home to setting an impressive table, I'll share with you some of my favorite entertaining tips. You'll also find tasty recipes such as jumbo prawns with feather-light crust, served with spicy mango chutney, grilled bison New York strip steaks with ancho glaze, chicken enchiladas with mole rojo, and Texas ribs with spiced dry rub and molasses brown sugar glaze. And for dessert, select from apple turnovers with vanilla bean syrup, Pavlova with raspberry sorbet and strawberries, banana and pecan Foster cake with buttercream frosting, and many more recipes you and your friends can enjoy together.

Photo from Christy's Scrapbook

Before Guests Arrive

I love to set the stage for a gathering long before guests arrive. If Randy and I are at *Swan's Nest*, that usually means the kitchen. Truth be told, we have two kitchens at *Swan's Nest*—the small, intimate kitchen where we cook our everyday meals in the space that was originally gold baron Ben Revett's office, with its gold vault directly adjacent—but that's another story—and the new studio kitchen Randy and I built onto the original house, where I film content for television shows and conduct photography sessions.

We've discovered that when entertaining in Dallas we tend to host our guests in the living room prior to dinner. We enjoy hors d'oeuvres and wine while seated on sofas around the coffee table, glistening with crystal rose bowls and candlelight. The atmosphere is elegant, gracious, and welcoming.

In Breckenridge, where life is more casual, guests prefer being invited into the kitchen to sip wine and watch the action as the finishing touches are added to the meal. With its oversize island counter, welcoming hearth, and magnificent mountain views, the studio kitchen is an ideal location to welcome guests and build anticipation for the forthcoming meal.

Here, I've created a first-course still life my guests will notice as soon as they arrive. The shiny black quartz island countertop creates a dramatic background for small square white plates, individual sauce bowls, and miniature silver forks. White linen cutwork napkins I found in Puerto Rico during a Caribbean cruise, overlapped and arranged in a diamond pattern, continue the black and white theme. Delicate, oversize wine glasses with tall, thin stems sparkle in the background, and floral arrangements add softness to the overall effect. While casual, there's still a feeling of graciousness that transcends the kitchen atmosphere and makes guests feel pampered, thanks to the striking black-and-white theme, beautiful glassware, elegant linens, flowers, and the forethought shown by the hosts. It's a formula that translates well to any home.

Jumbo Prawns with Feather-Light Crust

Rice flour and panko crumbs are the secret to these delicate, light-as-a-feather shrimp. Serve them as a main course, or as I have here—an easy-to-pick-up appetizer as guests gather in the kitchen around my island. The shrimp are delicious served with mango chutney or an Asian dipping sauce. **YIELDS 8 SERVINGS**

INGREDIENTS

1	cup rice flour
½	cup panko Japanese-style bread crumbs
1	teaspoon coarse sea salt
½	teaspoon freshly ground pepper mélange
2	eggs
1	tablespoon water
2	pounds raw jumbo shrimp, shelled, deveined, tail attached
	canola oil

In a shallow medium-size bowl, stir together rice flour, panko crumbs, salt, and pepper; set it aside.

In a small bowl, whip together the eggs and water with a fork.

Preheat a large skillet or wok over medium heat. Add oil to a depth of 1 inch. When the oil is hot, dip the shrimp into the egg wash and then into flour mixture until it is well coated. Transfer the shrimp to the skillet and cook 1½ minutes, flip them over, and cook 1½ minutes more, or until the shrimp are golden brown. Drain on paper towels and keep warm. Repeat the process with the remaining shrimp, working in small batches to accommodate the skillet size.

"An easy-to-pick up appetizer as guests gather in the kitchen around my island."

Spicy Mango Chutney

One of my favorite condiments is mango chutney. I love to serve it with pork roast, but here I've paired it with prawns for an Indian-inspired hors d'oeuvre that's terrific while guests are settling in for a festive evening, mingling and chatting over a glass of wine. This recipe was inspired by four of our Breckenridge, Colorado, neighbors. They've all spent time in India—one, Angel Caughey, was born there—so they love to cook Indian food, and sometimes Randy and I receive an invitation to join them.

I'm crazy about dinnerware and my cupboards are full of "eye candy" options, so I prefer to serve the chutney in miniature white bowls that show off the color and texture of this sweet and spicy condiment. I filled the bowls generously with chutney and place them on small, square appetizer plates, which when grouped en masse, create an artistic, culinary still life on the kitchen island. Once the feather-light shrimp is added, the party begins! YIELDS 3 CUPS CHUTNEY

INGREDIENTS

3	ripe mangos, peeled, seeded, and cut into ¼-inch cubes
2	tablespoons canola oil
2	cups sweet onion, peeled and finely chopped
½	teaspoon chile flakes
1	tablespoon cornstarch
½	cup plus 2 tablespoons tart apple cider
1	cup brown sugar, packed
2	tablespoons granulated sugar
1	tablespoon cider vinegar
2	teaspoons curry powder
½	teaspoon dry ginger
¼	teaspoon Saigon cinnamon

Preheat a medium saucepan over medium heat, add oil, and swirl to coat the bottom of the pan. Add onion and sauté 3 minutes or until it begins to soften; stir in the chile flakes.

Place the cornstarch in a small bowl and whisk in 2 tablespoons of the apple cider to form a smooth slurry; set it aside. Stir the remaining cider into the onion mixture and add brown sugar, granulated sugar, vinegar, curry powder, ginger, and cinnamon. Bring the mixture to a boil, stir in the mango and reserved cornstarch slurry, and cook 10 minutes, stirring frequently, until the mixture thickens and reduces by one-fourth.

Cocktail Meatballs with Spicy Cranberry Glaze

Mountain gatherings tend to be pretty casual affairs, so my *Swan's Nest* studio kitchen often plays an important role as the initial gathering spot for guests while I'm putting the finishing touches on the meal. I set up one side of my large kitchen island as an appetizer buffet with small, square white plates, forks, napkins, and garnishes. As soon as guests arrive, they can see I've planned something special for them, which sets the tone for a relaxed, enjoyable evening.

This tempting cocktail meatball dish allows guests to indulge while I'm busy in the kitchen. Panko crumbs keep the meatballs juicy inside, and the sauce is sweet, tangy, and vibrant. Best of all, the meatballs may be made several days ahead or frozen until the day of serving—a great time-saver for any host. YIELDS 65 MEATBALLS

INGREDIENTS

2	pounds ground chuck
1	cup panko Japanese bread crumbs
½	cup red onion, peeled and finely chopped
3	large cloves garlic, peeled and minced
1	teaspoon kosher salt
1	teaspoon onion powder
½	teaspoon freshly ground black pepper
½	teaspoon cayenne pepper
2	eggs

Preheat the oven to 350 degrees. In a large bowl, combine the meat, bread crumbs, onion, garlic, salt, onion powder, black pepper, cayenne pepper, and eggs. Mix well with a fork or hands, roll the mixture into 1-inch meatballs, and place them on large cookie sheets. Bake 12 minutes, turn the meatballs over, and bake 12 minutes more. Remove them from the oven, cool several minutes, and remove them from the trays.

Cranberry Glaze
INGREDIENTS

1	14-ounce can jellied cranberry sauce
1	14-ounce can whole cranberry sauce
1½	cups chili sauce
⅓	cup dry red wine
3	tablespoons brown sugar, packed
½	teaspoon Worchestershire sauce
3	shakes of Tabasco, or to taste

In a large saucepan over medium heat, stir together the cranberry sauces, chili sauce, wine, brown sugar, Worchestershire sauce, and Tabasco. Bring the mixture to a low boil, stirring frequently. Reduce the heat to low, add the meatballs, cover, and simmer 20 to 30 minutes, stirring occasionally, until the meatballs are hot.

Sea Scallops with Triple Sec-Orange Sauce and Mango Ponzu Salsa

For a quick meal with the caché of an elegant night out, this sautéed scallops dish is ideal for a family meal or a gathering with friends. I like to make the mango salsa ahead and allow the flavors to meld, which means dinner takes just minutes to fix when everyone is ready to dine. The ponzu lime sauce has a sweet and salty flavor so popular in today's cuisine, which adds a fresh twist to the mango salsa. When purchasing sea scallops, I look for wild caught, domestic scallops that have a fresh, white appearance. Allow five sea scallops per person for hearty appetites. YIELDS 2 SERVINGS

Salsa

INGREDIENTS

1   ripe mango, rinsed, peeled, pitted, and sliced into ½-inch cubes

2   tablespoons red onion, peeled and finely chopped

2   tablespoons orange bell pepper, rinsed, seeded, and chopped into ¼-inch pieces

1   tablespoon freshly squeezed lime juice

1   teaspoon ponzu citrus seasoning sauce with lime (I use Kikkoman)

1   tablespoon fresh cilantro, rinsed and chopped

In a medium bowl, combine the mango, onion, bell pepper, lime juice, ponzu sauce, and cilantro. Toss well, cover, and chill until ready to serve.

Sea Scallops

INGREDIENTS

½   pound sea scallops, about 10, rinsed and dried on paper towels

1   tablespoon olive oil

¼   cup triple sec

1   tablespoon freshly squeezed orange juice sea salt and freshly ground black pepper

½   tablespoon unsalted butter

4   thin orange slices, for garnish

Preheat a medium skillet over medium heat, add oil, and swirl to coat the bottom of the pan. Add the scallops and sauté them 4 to 5 minutes, without stirring, until the bottoms are golden brown. Turn them over and sauté 3 to 4 minutes more until they brown on the bottom and are firm to the touch.

Transfer the scallops to a platter and cover them to keep them warm. Deglaze the pan with triple sec and orange juice, stirring to loosen any brown bits, and cook until the liquid is reduced by half. Season the sauce with salt and pepper, remove the pan from the heat, add the butter, and stir gently until the butter has melted.

To serve, divide the scallops between two plates and garnish the plate with mango salsa. Pour the sauce over the scallops and arrange the orange slices between the scallops and the salsa.

Parties – Take Advantage Of Small Spaces

Children are particularly fond of playing in small spaces—a closet, staircase landing, or cozy nook in a room. I've decided adults are no different. During a party, they cram into the smallest kitchen space to sip wine, nibble on hors d'oeuvres, and converse, when a generously proportioned living room awaits just steps away.

Photo from Christy's Scrapbook

At *Swan's Nest*, we have the ideal small space adjacent to our older kitchen, and my guests love it! It's Ben Revett's gold vault, where Colorado's "gold dredge King" stored his fortune, and where Randy and I store our wine. This intimate space, originally made secure from gold thieves by stone walls two feet-thick and lined with brick, now features creamy cabinets with leaded glass, in-cabinet lighting, and racks for wine storage. Though it boasts just twenty-four feet of open floor space, the vault becomes party central whenever Randy and I host a cocktail or large dinner party. How ten adults can fit into that small space and stand there for almost an hour is beyond me. Sometimes I think it's the wine, or perhaps the room's rich history, but mostly I think it's the cozy atmosphere a small space creates.

For large parties, I take advantage of the vault's coziness and inevitable draw by making it the bar. On the counters, I arrange wine glasses, wine bottles, an ice bucket for chilling white wine and Champagne, corkscrew, napkins and several bowls of snacks. I find that guests take turns being the unofficial bartender, which allows them to spend more time in the vault, while freeing Randy to circulate among our guests. It's a win-win situation.

If your home features a small space that usually goes unused during gatherings, such as the laundry or mudroom, take advantage of this intimate area and transform it into the bar. Cover appliances with an attractive tablecloth or inexpensive, but luxurious fabric remnant, outfit the space with a small table or cart, trays of glassware, wine and cocktail accoutrements, and a small decorative lamp to provide soft, romantic lighting. Then stand back and watch the magic happen. Before long, your guests will be drawn to this completely transformed, cozy space, and your party will be a huge success.

...the vault becomes party central whenever Randy and I host a cocktail or large dinner party."

Strawberry and Blackberry Garden Salad with Dark Sweet Cherry Balsamic Vinaigrette

I've really embraced the variety of flavored balsamic vinegars that are now becoming more widely available in specialty stores and supermarkets. Their intense flavors—some sweet and others savory—add new flavor dimensions to so many recipes, from entrees to desserts.

When sweet and juicy spring and summer berries are abundant, this fruity salad is a beautiful first course or side salad. The contrast of red and black sweet berries and red leaf lettuce is simple, but stunning, and the sweet, tangy dark cherry vinaigrette provides a delightfully refreshing taste experience. For small gatherings, arrange the salad on individual plates, but when expecting a crowd, increase the amount of ingredients, double or triple the vinaigrette, and serve the salad on a large, white platter. For an entrée salad, add strips of poached chicken and red onion rings. YIELDS 4 SERVINGS

INGREDIENTS

1	bunch red leaf lettuce, rinsed, spun dry, 4 leaves whole, the remainder torn
1	pint fresh strawberries, rinsed, hulled, and sliced
6	ounces fresh blackberries, rinsed
1	tablespoon dark sweet cherry balsamic vinegar (I use Pasta Moré)
3	tablespoons extra virgin olive oil
	kosher salt and freshly ground black pepper, to taste

Place a lettuce leaf on each salad plate and top with torn lettuce. Arrange sliced strawberries over the lettuce and garnish the salad with blackberries. Chill until ready to serve.

Just before serving, combine balsamic vinegar, olive oil, salt, and pepper in a small bowl. Whisk gently to mix and spoon the vinaigrette over the berries and lettuce.

Spring Medley Salad

Each summer in Dillon, Colorado, the farmers market opens for another season. Situated with a view of 12,000 foot tall mountain peaks still capped in winter snow, and just a brief walk from Lake Dillon where sail boats skim across the water, the market features farmers from Colorado's Eastern plains and Western Slope who make the long drive through the mountains to sell their fresh produce, homemade sausages, locally-produced lamb and bison, artisan breads, jams, flowers, and fragrant herbs for Summit County locals and tourists. There, I've discovered purple-red beet greens, some of the prettiest rainbow Swiss chard I've ever seen, and an unusual, dainty speckled salad green called "Flash Trout Back." I've purchased herbs for my garden, flavored vinegars for salads, meats, and desserts, locally raised lamb, German sausages, squash blossoms, freshly-roasted chili peppers, assorted vegetables, and a dazzling array of organic salad greens.

I return home to *Swan's Nest* after my trip to the market, my canvas bags bulging with new discoveries, my mind filled with inspiration, and my appetite whetted. The experience reminds me of my weekly visits to the marchè while we lived in Paris.

This composed salad is a result of one day's excursion to the Dillon Farmers Market. The attractive display of assorted greens, sugar snap peas, colorful pear tomatoes, and fragrant herbs so fresh from their recent harvest will definitely make your family and guests sit up and take notice. It's an artistic rendering of spring and summer's bounteous produce, arranged on a large platter and dressed to impress. YIELDS 8 TO 10 SERVINGS

INGREDIENTS

8	small red new potatoes
¼	pound sugar snap peas, rinsed and trimmed
1	small bunch red leaf lettuce, rinsed and spun dry
1	small bunch baby leaf spinach, rinsed and spun dry
1	small bunch baby beet greens or other local salad greens, rinsed and spun dry
1	14-ounce can artichoke hearts, drained and quartered
¾	cup red pear tomatoes, rinsed
¾	cup yellow pear tomatoes, rinsed
2	thick slices red onion, peeled and divided into rings

3	sprigs fresh basil, rinsed and julienned
2	sprigs fresh marjoram, rinsed and chopped
2	cloves garlic, peeled and finely chopped
1	teaspoon Dijon mustard
3	tablespoons fig balsamic vinegar
½	cup olive oil
	coarse salt and freshly ground pepper
2	tablespoons capers, drained but not rinsed
	Parmigiano-Reggiano, shaved, for garnish

Rinse the potatoes and place them in a medium saucepan with enough water to cover them. Cover, bring the water to a boil over high heat, then reduce the heat to medium-low and cook until they are knife tender. Drain, transfer them to a bowl, cover, and chill until ready to use.

Place the sugar snap peas in a saucepan and add water to a depth of ½ inch. Cover, bring the water to a boil over high heat, reduce the heat to medium-low, and cook just until they are crisp-tender, about 3 to 4 minutes. Drain and plunge the snap peas into an ice water bath to stop the cooking process.

Slice the red potatoes ¼-inch thick. Arrange the lettuce, spinach, and beet greens on a large platter and top with potatoes, sugar snap peas, artichoke hearts, pear tomatoes, and rings of red onion. Sprinkle with fresh basil and marjoram.

In a medium bowl, stir together the garlic, mustard, and balsamic vinegar. Gently whisk in the olive oil, salt, and pepper just until the vinaigrette is blended; stir in the capers. Spoon the vinaigrette over the salad and garnish with shavings of Parmigiano-Reggiano.

French Lentil and Belgian Endive Salad

French lentils are a dried, green legume favored by the ancient Greeks. They're packed with flavor and nutrition, and when cooked and chilled, lentils are an excellent choice to add tasty variety to summer salads. In this recipe, I've combined French lentils with crunchy red onion and celery, salty and chewy Kalamata olives, yellow cherry tomatoes for color and sweetness, and Belgian endive as a garnish for its impressive, pale-yellow-and-white long spears and slight bitterness, all tossed in a light and tangy red wine vinaigrette. I like to serve this beautiful salad in a deep glass trifle bowl with the endive spears standing upright around the edges and the lentil mixture mounded within. YIELDS 12 SERVINGS

 TIP: At high altitude, dried lentils take extra time to become tender when cooked. Please add 10 to 15 minutes to the cooking time specified below.

INGREDIENTS

2½	cups green lentils
4	cups chicken or vegetable stock
1¼	cups water
1	teaspoon kosher salt
¾	cup celery, rinsed and chopped
½	cup red onion, peeled and chopped
1	large or 2 small Belgian endive, outer spears removed for garnish
¼	cup pitted Kalamata olives, sliced
24	yellow cherry tomatoes, rinsed and halved
1½	teaspoons Dijon mustard (I prefer Maille)
3	tablespoons red wine vinegar
½	cup olive oil
	kosher salt and freshly ground black pepper, to taste

In a large saucepan or Dutch oven, stir together lentils, chicken stock, water, and salt. Bring the mixture to a boil, cover, reduce the heat to medium-low, and cook 45 to 50 minutes, or until the liquid is absorbed and the lentils are tender. Remove it from the heat, cool, and transfer it to a large bowl.

Add celery and onion, and toss gently. Remove the outer spears from the Belgian endive and reserve them for garnish. Coarsely chop the remaining endive and stir it into the lentils with the olives and cherry tomatoes.

In a small bowl, combine Dijon mustard and vinegar. Gently whisk in the oil, season the mixture with salt and pepper, and pour the vinaigrette over the lentils. Toss gently to mix and transfer the salad to a serving bowl. Cover and chill until ready to serve. Just before serving, insert the spears of endive along the rim of the serving bowl for garnish.

Pan-Seared Cod with Baby Spinach and Roasted Red Pepper Coulis

Often the most impressive dishes are a combination of quick and easy recipes, layered to create a beautiful balance of appearance, flavors, and textures. This cod dish is a prime example. The fish is pan sautéed, then is plated in a pool of sweet and spicy red bell pepper coulis and garnished with wilted fresh spinach. I prepare the coulis earlier in the day or even a day or two ahead, so my final dinner preparation takes just minutes.

YIELDS 2 SERVINGS

INGREDIENTS

2	tablespoons unsalted butter
1½	tablespoons olive oil
¾	pound fresh cod, rinsed and dried on paper towel
¼	teaspoon Mediterranean sea salt
¼	teaspoon freshly ground black pepper
½	cup dry white wine
4	ounces fresh baby spinach
2	lemon wedges, for garnish

Preheat a large skillet over medium heat. Add butter and olive oil, and heat until the butter has melted. Cut the fish into two equal portions and season it on both sides with salt and pepper. Place both pieces of fish in the pan, tucking the thinner portion under so both pieces of fish cook evenly. Cook 4 to 5 minutes until the bottom of the fish is lightly browned, turn it over, and cook 2 to 3 minutes more, or until it flakes. Remove the fish from the pan and cover to keep it warm.

Deglaze the pan with wine, scraping up any brown bits with a wooden spoon. Cook until the liquid is reduced by half, add the spinach, and sauté just until it is wilted, about 1 minute. Season the spinach with a dash of salt.

To serve, heat the red pepper coulis in a small saucepan just until it is hot. Spoon a pool of coulis into the center of two plates, place a piece of fish in the center of the coulis, and garnish each with wilted spinach. Pour any remaining pan juices over the fish and garnish with a lemon wedge.

Roasted Red Pepper Coulis

It's easy to create a little gourmet magic in your kitchen when you want to impress your family or guests. Whip up this zesty sauce early in the day in a blender, then heat just before serving. Once the fish is cooked, spoon a pool of pepper coulis onto the plate and arrange the fish on top. The coulis is also delicious stirred into pasta.

There's nothing like the taste of freshly-roasted peppers, but when time is short or red bell peppers are unavailable, substitute prepared roasted red peppers, available in jars in the grocery section of your favorite supermarket. YIELDS 1 CUP

INGREDIENTS

2	large red bell peppers, rinsed and dried
2	tablespoons sweet onion, peeled and chopped
1½	tablespoons olive oil
1	teaspoon red wine vinegar
¼	teaspoon kosher salt
¼	teaspoon freshly ground black pepper
1/8	teaspoon cayenne pepper
4-6	drops Tabasco sauce, optional

Preheat the oven to 400 degrees. Place the peppers on a cookie sheet lined with parchment paper and roast them in the oven 20 to 25 minutes, turning them occasionally, until they are blackened. Remove them from the oven, cool 10 minutes, and place them into a plastic zipper bag to steam. When they are cool, peel the skin, remove the stems and seeds, and discard.

Place the peppers, onion, olive oil, vinegar, salt, black pepper, cayenne pepper, and Tabasco in a blender, cover, and purée until the sauce is smooth. Serve immediately or cover and chill overnight.

Onion Strings

There's no need to visit a steak house to enjoy onion strings, because these are easy to make at home. Thin, crisp onion strings are the dressed-up version of country-style onion rings, and they're an impressive way to garnish grilled beef or bison steaks, burgers, and quail. Paper-thin slices of sweet onion are soaked in buttermilk, separated into strings, dipped into flour, and deep-fried for just a few moments until they become crisp and golden brown. They're mouthwatering, positively addictive, and so hard to resist, they may never make it to the plate! YIELDS 4 SERVINGS

INGREDIENTS

1	large sweet onion, peeled and sliced paper-thin
1	cup buttermilk
2	cups flour
1	tablespoon onion powder
2	teaspoons kosher salt
	freshly ground black pepper, to taste
½	teaspoon cayenne pepper
3	cups canola or grape seed oil

Place the onion slices in a large, plastic zipper bag and pour in the buttermilk. Close the bag and marinate the onions at least 1 hour.

Just before serving, preheat a large skillet over medium heat, add the oil, and heat it to 375 degrees. In a large bowl, stir together flour, onion powder, salt, black pepper, and cayenne pepper until they are well mixed. Preheat a large skillet over medium heat, add the oil, and heat it to 375 degrees.

Remove some of the onions from the buttermilk, toss them into the flour mixture, shake off any excess flour, and carefully drop them into the hot oil. Fry just until they are golden brown, remove them with tongs, and drain on a platter covered with paper towels. Repeat the process until all the onions are cooked, adjusting the temperature if necessary.

"They're mouthwatering, positively addictive, and so hard to resist, they may never make it to the plate!"

Grilled Bison New York Strip Steaks with Ancho Glaze

As my husband Randy and I embraced living in the mountains, I began to explore local ingredients—some of which have been on Western tables since early times. Serving bison is a way to connect with the West, our country's history, and with the land.

Grass-fed bison is readily found in Colorado grocery stores and meat markets, and while not available throughout the country, I've seen cuts of bison in Pittsburgh, Pennsylvania supermarkets. Bison is lower in fat, calories, and cholesterol than similar cuts of beef, so it's a good protein choice for those on low-fat diets. Bison New York strip steak is best served medium-rare.

This is a recipe I created for a mountain food and wine event, and I knew I'd struck gold when I saw guests' eyes light up as they discovered they were about to sample bison. For many, it was their first exposure to this still-unfamiliar protein, and the compliments poured in. The best recommendations came from guests who walked from one end of the event to the other because "I heard the bison is not-to-be-missed!" Here, it is served with a robust ancho chili sauce that's really tasty with beef and chicken, too.

YIELDS 4 TO 6 SERVINGS

INGREDIENTS

2   large bison New York strip steaks (1½-inch thickness)

    coarse salt and freshly ground black pepper

Ancho Glaze

3   dried ancho chiles, about 1 ounce total

1¼   cups boiling water

1   tablespoon canola oil

¼   cup onion, peeled and finely chopped

2   large cloves garlic, peeled and finely chopped

¼   cup honey

3   tablespoons ketchup

1   tablespoon molasses

1   tablespoon brown sugar, packed

1   tablespoon orange zest

¼   teaspoon coarse salt

¼   teaspoon freshly ground black pepper

⅛   teaspoon crushed red pepper flakes

YIELDS 1 CUP

Place the chiles in a medium heat-proof bowl, add boiling water, and cover the chiles with a small plate to keep them submerged. Soak them 30 minutes until they have softened. Transfer the chiles to a cutting board, reserving the soaking liquid. Remove the stems and seeds, and discard. Coarsely chop the chiles and set them aside.

Preheat a small saucepan over medium heat, add the oil, and swirl to coat the bottom of the pan. Add onions and cook 4 to 5 minutes until they have softened, stirring often. Add the garlic, cook 1 minute, and stir in the reserved ancho chiles.

Stir in honey, ketchup, molasses, brown sugar, orange zest, salt, pepper, and red pepper flakes. Cook the mixture 5 to 8 minutes until the flavors have blended, adding 1 or 2 tablespoons of the chile soaking liquid if the sauce becomes too thick. Remove the pan from the heat and set it aside 10 minutes to cool. Transfer the mixture to a food processor and process until it is smooth, adding 6 to 7 tablespoons of the chili soaking liquid until the glaze is the desired consistency.

Bison Steaks

Preheat the grill until it is hot. Season both sides of the meat generously with salt and pepper, transfer it to the grill, and cook 4 to 5 minutes. Turn the meat over and cook 4 to 5 minutes more. For medium rare, turn the meat again and cook 2 minutes more on each side, or until it is the desired degree of doneness. Transfer the meat to a cutting board, cover it to keep warm, and allow it to rest 10 minutes.

To serve, slice the meat at an angle into thick slices and garnish with chile glaze.

Grilled Smokey Hanger Steak Soft Tacos with Caramelized Onions and Jalapeños

Beef hanger steaks are becoming more popular in the U.S. and are prized for their flavor. Derived from the sternum area, the hanger steak lies behind the more familiar skirt steak often used for fajitas, but is considered more flavorful. Marinating the hanger steak for an hour or two before grilling helps to tenderize it. To cook, grill the meat over a hot fire until it's medium-rare, and slice it thinly at an angle.

In this recipe, dry spices, smoked paprika, and Liquid Smoke are blended into the marinade to lend rustic flavor. Caramelized onions cooked with jalapeños add sweetness and a bit of heat.

This simple, flavorful dish can be the basis for fun, backyard gatherings with family or friends. Add a Western flair with a red checked tablecloth and bandana cloth napkins, or opt for a Tex-Mex feeling by accessorizing the table with bright yellows and hot pinks and blues. Fill a galvanized tub with ice and longneck Texas beers, or quench thirsts with pitchers of icy-cold margaritas. For the kids, I fill pitchers with cold lemonade and have glasses ready with a small pool of strawberry or blackberry syrup in the bottom of each one so kids have a special treat, too! YIELDS 4 SERVINGS

"*In this recipe, dry spices, smoked paprika, and Liquid Smoke are blended into the marinade to lend rustic flavor. Caramelized onions cooked with jalapeños add sweetness and a bit of heat.*"

INGREDIENTS

1½	pounds beef hanger steak
3	tablespoons canola or grape seed oil
1	teaspoon onion powder
½	teaspoon smoked paprika
½	teaspoon smoked sea salt flakes (I use Maldon)
½	teaspoon Liquid Smoke
¼	teaspoon cumin
¼	teaspoon freshly ground black pepper
1	tablespoon olive oil
3	large sweet onions, such as Texas 1015 or Vidalia, peeled and sliced
1	large jalapeño, rinsed, seeded, and chopped juice of ½ fresh lime sprigs of fresh cilantro, for garnish
10	7-inch flour tortillas, wrapped in foil and heated

In a large plastic zipper bag, mix canola oil, onion powder, smoked paprika, sea salt, Liquid Smoke, cumin, and black pepper. Add the hanger steak, close the bag, rub the spice mixture into the meat, and chill 1 to 2 hours, or until shortly before cooking.

Thirty minutes before serving, preheat a large skillet over medium heat, add olive oil, and swirl to coat the bottom of the pan. Add sliced onions and cook 20 to 30 minutes, stirring occasionally, until the onions are golden brown. Stir in the jalapeño and cook 5 minutes more, or until it has softened.

While the onions are caramelizing, preheat the grill to medium-high heat. When it is hot, remove the meat from the marinade and place it on the grill. Cook 4 to 5 minutes until the bottom of the meat is well-seared, turn it over, and cook the other side 4 to 5 minutes. Turn the meat again and cook 2 to 3 minutes on each side, depending on the thickness, until a meat thermometer inserted into the center registers 135 degrees for medium-rare.

Remove the meat from the grill, transfer it to a cutting board, squeeze fresh lime juice onto the meat, cover it loosely with foil, and set it aside 10 minutes to rest. Slice the meat thinly at an angle, place it on a platter, and garnish it with the caramelized onion-jalapeño mixture and sprigs of fresh cilantro. To serve, spoon some of the meat and onion mixture into warm flour tortillas.

A Springtime Table Setting

After years of traveling around the country and speaking with audiences, I've learned many people believe the key to being a successful host lies in being a great cook. It's no wonder so many are reluctant to entertain at home. That's a lot of pressure for anyone, but particularly those who feel less confident in the kitchen.

I have always believed and taught that it's not the food that makes a successful gathering—it's the sheer joy of being together and the little things a host does to make guests comfortable and the gathering memorable. Setting a beautiful table is one of those things.

When Randy and I were married, it was a common practice for dinnerware, glassware, and flatware to match. Brides and grooms registered for sets of china, crystal, and silver that would create a seamless, "perfect" table setting. Fast-forward several decades, and we've come to realize that some of the most glorious, impressive, creative, and memorable tables are the result of mixing and matching colors, shapes, textures, and heights.

I'm rarely happier than when I'm setting a table. It makes my creative juices flow as I envision a setting that will elicit oohs and aahs from my guests. Every table setting begins with a blank slate, and I never know what the finished table will look like until I combine all the elements. I start by considering the season, a particular color I wish to use, or a special occasion that will be commemorated. Next, I open all my cupboards and take inventory of my collection of chargers, dishes, glasses, table linens, candlesticks, and accent pieces. Often, my table setting is influenced by a particularly beautiful or interesting textile, a whimsical salad plate, or a colorful piece of glass.

The springtime table setting pictured here began with the robin's egg blue salad plates. Their sculpted, flower-petal edges created flow in the design, so I chose white, beaded, square placemats I found at an estate sale to offset the curve. On top of the placemats, I layered large, glass chargers with a soft-blue spiral, white-on-white china dinner plates, and finally the salad plates that inspired the entire design.

The look was delicate, so I complemented the setting with etched water and wine glasses from our set of wedding crystal, and mixed them with antique, etched crystal juice glasses found in a nearby consignment store. Their slender shape made them a lovely substitute for champagne flutes. Antique champagne coupes, a cherished gift from my sister and brother-in-law Susan and Mark, held fresh fruit for an easy, but elegant first course. Floating candles, stemless wine glasses filled with spring blossoms, and fan-folded, antique damask linen napkins completed this lovely seasonal table setting.

"Every table setting begins with a blank slate, and I never know what the finished table will look like until I combine all the elements."

Orange-Glazed Roasted Duck Breasts

This fragrant, savory dish is fabulous, but your family and guests will never know how easy it is unless you tell them. The duck is scored in a diamond pattern and seared in a skillet, then roasted in the oven for about thirty minutes until the meat is tender and pink inside. Shortly before it's done, the meat is coated with an orange marmalade and Cointreau sauce that creates a heavenly glaze. For a gathering with friends, a romantic dinner with your sweetheart, or a special occasion, this impressive dish will be the highlight of your celebration. YIELDS 4 SERVINGS

INGREDIENTS

4   boneless duckling breasts

Kosher salt and freshly ground black pepper, to taste

½   cup Cointreau or other orange-flavor liqueur

½   cup beef stock or broth

4   tablespoons orange marmalade

        juice of 1 orange

1   orange, rinsed and thinly sliced, for garnish

"...this impressive dish will be the highlight of your celebration."

Preheat the oven to 400 degrees. Rinse the duck and dry them with paper towels. Using a sharp knife, trim excess skin as needed and score the skin to form a diamond pattern, taking care not to pierce the meat. Season both sides of the meat well with salt and pepper.

Preheat a large skillet over medium heat. Place the duck breasts, skin side down, in the skillet and cook 8 to 10 minutes until the skin is brown and crisp, draining excess fat as needed. Turn the meat over and cook 3 to 5 minutes more to sear it.

Transfer the meat to a roasting pan, reserving the skillet for the sauce, and roast the meat uncovered for 20 minutes. While the meat roasts, drain the fat from the skillet and place the pan over medium heat. When it is hot, deglaze the pan with Cointreau and beef stock, scraping up any brown bits from the bottom of the pan. Add orange marmalade and orange juice, stir well, and cook until the liquid is reduced by half. Season the sauce with black pepper.

During the final 10 minutes of roasting, spoon the sauce over the duck and cook until the meat is tender and light pink inside. Remove the meat from the oven, cover it with foil, and set it aside 10 minutes to rest. To serve, slice the meat at an angle and fan it out on dinner plates. Spoon any remaining juices next to the meat, garnish with a slice of orange, and serve.

Black Japonica Rice

Black Japonica is a blend of black and mahogany rice, available in specialty stores and some supermarkets. It has a nutty, earthy flavor and a pleasant, chewy texture. For buffets, this dark grain, accented with green onions and golden sultanas, provides a somewhat surprising deep, black color that's an exquisite contrast to duck, grilled meats, or fish. YIELDS 6 SERVINGS

INGREDIENTS

2¾   cups chicken broth
1   cup black japonica rice
      kosher salt
1   tablespoon olive oil
½   cup green onion, white and green parts, chopped
1   stalk celery, rinsed, ¼-inch dice
⅓   cup golden raisins
1   tablespoon olive oil
      freshly ground black pepper
1   tablespoon fresh marjoram, rinsed, stemmed, and chopped

In a large saucepan over high heat, stir together the broth, rice, and ¼ teaspoon salt. Bring the mixture to a boil, reduce the heat to low, and cover. Cook 40 to 45 minutes or until the liquid has been absorbed and the rice is tender.

Preheat a small skillet over medium heat, add the oil, and swirl to coat the bottom of the pan. Add onion, celery, and golden raisins, and cook 3 to 4 minutes, stirring frequently, until the vegetables are soft. Add marjoram and season the mixture with salt and pepper to taste.

Fluff the rice with a fork and gently stir in the vegetable herb mixture. Spoon the rice into a bowl or platter and serve.

Mushrooms in Sherry Cream Sauce

Fresh white mushrooms, combined with a few simple ingredients and a splash of dry sherry, become an elegant, no-fuss side dish that bakes in the oven while the final touches are added to a meal. The creamy broth surrounding the mushrooms is so rich and flavorful, it could also be used as a delicate sauce for sautéed veal or chicken breasts. Your guests will rave about this fabulous dish! YIELDS 6 TO 8 SERVINGS

INGREDIENTS

2	tablespoons unsalted butter
½	cup sweet onion, peeled and finely chopped
3	large cloves garlic, peeled and minced
2-3	tablespoons dry sherry
1	cup heavy cream
¼	cup vegetable broth
¼	teaspoon kosher salt
¼	teaspoon white pepper
1	pound white mushrooms, cleaned and halved
1	tablespoon fresh parsley, rinsed and chopped, for garnish

Preheat the oven to 350 degrees. In a large saucepan over medium heat, melt butter, add the onion, and sauté 3 minutes until the onion is soft. Add garlic and sauté 1 minute more until it is fragrant.

Stir in sherry, heavy cream, and vegetable broth. Bring the mixture to a boil and season it with salt and pepper. Remove the pan from the heat, add mushrooms, and stir gently until they are well coated. Transfer the mixture to a casserole dish, sprinkle with parsley, cover, and bake 30 minutes until it is hot and bubbly.

Photo from Christy's Scrapbook

Brussels Sprouts with Pan-Toasted Pine Nuts

Brussels sprouts, sweet onion, salty capers, and crunchy, toasted pine nuts combine for a deliciously easy vegetable side dish that moves beyond holiday meals. Guests love this pretty vegetable when I serve it with roasted meats or chicken. YIELDS 4 SERVINGS

INGREDIENTS

½	pound Brussels sprouts, rinsed
1	tablespoon olive oil
½	cup sweet onion, peeled and finely chopped
¼	cup pine nuts
2	tablespoons capers
2	large cloves garlic, peeled and chopped
1	tablespoons unsalted butter
	sea salt and freshly ground black pepper, to taste

Trim and quarter the Brussels sprouts. Transfer them to a steamer basket placed inside a medium saucepan filled with 1 inch water. Cover, bring the water to a boil, reduce the heat to medium, and steam the Brussels sprouts 5 minutes or until they are crisp-tender when pierced with a sharp knife.

Preheat a large skillet over medium heat, add oil, and swirl to coat the bottom of the pan. Add onion and pine nuts, and sauté 3 minutes until the onion is soft and the pine nuts are lightly toasted. Add Brussels sprouts and capers, and cook 3 minutes, stirring often. Stir in garlic and cook 1 minute more. Add butter, season the mixture with salt and pepper, and toss gently.

"*Guests love this pretty vegetable when I serve it with roasted meats or chicken.*"

Cheesy Cauliflower Bake

I created this luscious vegetable side dish with its silky cheese sauce for a *Swan's Nest* autumn dinner party with our Breckenridge friends the Caugheys and Wickerts. We were all gathered in my studio kitchen sipping wine and nibbling on appetizers while I moved between the stovetop and ovens, putting the final touches on the meal.

Once the cauliflower was partially steamed, I invited Al Wicket to stir together the cheese sauce, a task he happily accepted. Butter, flour, half-and-half, and Cheddar cheese combine for this dreamy sauce that is poured over the cauliflower and baked. It was only when the meal was served that Liz Wickert mentioned this dish is a British tradition she grew up with. We all loved it, but bringing back a favorite memory for Liz gave this dish special significance for me. YIELDS 6 TO 8 SERVINGS

INGREDIENTS

1	large head of cauliflower, rinsed, trimmed, and cut into large florets
¼	cup unsalted butter
2	tablespoons flour
1¾	cups half-and-half
2	teaspoons dry mustard
	kosher salt and freshly ground black pepper, to taste
1½	cups medium Cheddar cheese, grated
⅛	teaspoon paprika, for garnish

Preheat the oven to 350 degrees and spray a casserole dish with nonstick vegetable spray. Rinse the cauliflower, remove the outer leaves, and cut it into florets. Transfer the florets to a large saucepan, add water to a depth of ¾ inch, cover, and steam until the cauliflower is barely knife tender. Remove it from the heat, drain, place the cauliflower in the casserole dish, and set it aside.

Melt the butter in a large saucepan over medium heat and whisk in the flour. Cook 2 minutes, whisking constantly. Add the half-and-half a little at a time and the dry mustard, whisking constantly until the sauce is smooth and starts to thicken. Add the cheese, ½ cup at a time, whisking until the cheese has melted and the sauce is smooth and creamy. Season the sauce with salt and pepper, and pour it over the cauliflower. Sprinkle with paprika, cover, and bake 30 minutes, or until the casserole is hot and the cauliflower is knife tender.

Sautéed Cabbage, Endive and Radicchio

I owe my husband Randy the credit for this one. He was cleaning out the fridge a few days before we left *Swan's Nest,* and he found a head of green cabbage, a Vidalia onion, a red endive, and some radicchio. When stirred together with sweet soy sauce and tart wine vinegar, this quick vegetable dish is colorful, fragrant, and incredibly addictive. I've added celery seeds to produce an extra flavor component. YIELDS 4 SERVINGS

ONE PREPARATION NOTE: Red endive loses it color quickly when sautéed, so add it toward the end of the recipe to maintain its pretty color.

INGREDIENTS

1½	tablespoons olive oil
½	large sweet onion, peeled and coarsely chopped
½	head green cabbage, rinsed and coarsely chopped
1	cup radicchio, rinsed and coarsely chopped
2	tablespoons soy sauce (I use Kikkoman)
1	tablespoon red wine vinegar
1	red endive, sliced cross-wise
3	large cloves garlic, peeled and finely chopped
½	teaspoon celery seeds
	freshly ground black pepper, to taste

Preheat a large skillet over medium heat, add the oil, and swirl to coat the bottom of the pan. Add onion and sauté until it is golden brown. Add cabbage and radicchio, and sauté until the cabbage is crisp-tender, about 4 minutes.

Stir in soy sauce, vinegar, endive, garlic, celery seeds, and pepper. Reduce the heat to medium-low, cover, and cook the mixture 5 to 6 minutes, stirring occasionally, or until it is hot and fragrant.

Brown Sugar-Curried Sweet Potato Casserole

Here's a twist on baked sweet potatoes that I like to serve during buffet dinner parties. I peel and thinly slice sweet potatoes into a pretty casserole dish, then pour a brown sugar and honey-sweetened curry sauce over the potatoes just before baking. Easy and delicious! YIELDS 6 TO 8 SERVINGS

 TIP: Sweet potatoes take much longer to cook at high altitude than in my Dallas kitchen. Slice the potatoes very thin, increase the oven temperature to 400 degrees, and bake the casserole 60 to 90 minutes until the sweet potatoes are knife tender.

INGREDIENTS

1½ pounds sweet potatoes, rinsed, peeled, and sliced ⅛-inch thick
3   tablespoons honey
2   tablespoons tart apple cider
1   teaspoon curry powder
1   tablespoon brown sugar, packed
¼   teaspoon kosher salt
    freshly ground black pepper, to taste

Preheat the oven to 375 degrees and place the sweet potatoes in a large mixing bowl.

In a small bowl, stir together honey, apple cider, curry powder, brown sugar, salt, and pepper. Pour the mixture over the sweet potatoes and toss gently until the potatoes are well coated. Transfer them to a medium casserole dish, cover, and bake 45 to 60 minutes, or until the sweet potatoes are knife tender.

As summer turns to fall and the markets are filled with newly-harvested varieties of squash, I purchase extras to use as decorations for the mantle over our fireplace. I combine them with silk autumn leaf garland, small pumpkins, fragrant apples, and a string of tiny clear lights that glows softly each evening. It's a simple, but gracious way to welcome the beauty and bounty of autumn indoors. To protect the mantle, cover it with a moisture-proof cloth before decorating with fresh produce.

French Country Chicken with Cranberries and Artichokes

I learned while Randy and I lived in France that the French possess a wonderful ability to celebrate each day around the table. I believe some of this celebratory spirit stems from the French tradition of shopping each day for food, selecting only what they need for the day's meal. This daily ritual creates an intimate connection with their food, which is often purchased from shop keepers they've known for years. The result is a leisurely, joyous gathering around the table.

I love this recipe because it reminds me of the simple goodness so often found in French cooking. Chicken thighs are sautéed until they're tender and brown, then served with a tasty onion-leek Marsala wine sauce that captures every bit of flavor from the savory pan juices. Dried cranberries plump as they cook, adding a nice chewy texture, and artichoke hearts provide panache to this otherwise humble dish. YIELDS 4 TO 6 SERVINGS

INGREDIENTS

1½	tablespoons olive oil
8	skinless chicken thighs, rinsed and patted dry
	kosher salt and freshly ground black pepper, to taste
1	leek, rinsed and chopped, white part only
⅓	cup red onion, peeled and finely chopped
¼	cup dried cranberries
2	large cloves garlic, peeled and finely chopped
½	cup Marsala wine
½	cup chicken stock or broth
1	cup artichoke hearts, drained and cut into quarters
1	sprig fresh rosemary, rinsed, stemmed, and chopped
	fresh rosemary sprigs, for garnish

Preheat a large skillet over medium heat, add oil, and swirl to coat the bottom of the pan. Season the chicken with salt and pepper, and place them, smooth side down, in the skillet. Sauté 3 minutes or until the chicken is brown, then turn them over and cook 3 minutes more. Cook an additional 6 to 9 minutes, turning the meat as needed, until a meat thermometer registers 165 degrees when inserted into the center of the meat. Transfer the meat to a warm platter and cover it to keep it warm.

Add the leek and onion to the skillet and sauté 1 minute until they soften. Stir in cranberries and garlic, and cook 1 minute more. Deglaze the pan with wine and chicken stock, stirring well to loosen the brown bits from the bottom of the pan. Bring the liquid to a boil and cook until it has reduced by half. Add artichoke hearts and chopped rosemary, stir gently, and cook just until the artichokes are heated through. Season the sauce with salt and pepper, spoon it over the chicken, and garnish the platter with sprigs of fresh rosemary.

Grilled Moroccan Lamb Kabobs with Tzatziki

I love making kabobs for backyard cookouts and veranda parties. They're easy to assemble in advance, take just minutes to cook, provide a bit of the all-important "wow"
factor, and are fun to eat. Add Middle Eastern spices that tingle the taste buds and a
creamy yogurt and cucumber dip to cool the spices, and your cookout is sure to be a
sensation. I created this recipe for a Colorado summertime culinary event with a guest
list of five hundred, but tried it out first on our Breckenridge neighbors, Liz and Al
Wickert and Angel and Curt Caughey. It was a hit with our neighbors and the Snow-
mass culinary festival crowd, many of whom returned multiple times for "one more
taste." Try it for your next party! YIELDS 20 TO 22 KABOBS

Kabobs

INGREDIENTS

1½	teaspoons ground coriander
1	teaspoon cumin
½	teaspoon Saigon cinnamon
½	teaspoon coarse salt
½	teaspoon freshly ground black pepper
4	small zucchini squash, rinsed and cut into ½ -inch thickness
3	pounds boneless lamb sirloin, cut into 1-inch cubes
2	large red onions, peeled and sliced into 1-inch pieces
½	cup olive oil
	bamboo skewers, soaked 24 hours in water

In a small bowl, stir together the coriander, cumin, cinnamon,
salt, and pepper; set the mixture aside. Thread a slice of squash
onto each skewer, piercing the green skin to add stability during
cooking. Add a cube of lamb and slices of red onion. Continue
the pattern until all of the ingredients have been used. Brush
the kabobs lightly on all sides with olive oil and sprinkle lightly
with the reserved spice mixture. Cover and chill the kabobs until
ready to cook.

Preheat the grill to medium heat. Place the kabobs on the grill
and cook, turning occasionally, until the vegetables are tender
and the meat is still pink inside, about 10 to 15 minutes, depending on the grill. Serve with a generous dollop of tzatziki sauce
garnished with a sprinkle of fresh mint.

Tzatziki

INGREDIENTS

2   8-ounce containers Greek or plain yogurt

2   cucumbers, peeled, seeded, and finely chopped

3   cloves garlic, peeled and minced

½   teaspoon coarse salt

¼   teaspoon white pepper

2   tablespoons chopped fresh mint

1   lemon, juiced

In a large bowl, stir together the yogurt, cucumbers, garlic, salt, pepper, and fresh mint. Add lemon juice and stir well. Cover and chill at least 2 hours before serving to allow flavors to meld.

YIELDS 3 CUPS

Texas Ribs with Spiced Dry Rub and Molasses Brown Sugar Glaze

Summer is brief in the mountains. One moment, there's snow on the ground, and then the snow is gone and wild flowers are blooming everywhere, as if they know their beautiful display will be cut short by an early fall. So, as soon as temperatures warm enough to dine outdoors, we fire up the grill and invite friends for dinner on the veranda with breathtaking views of the Tenmile Range.

We love to spend our summers in Colorado, but I like to bring a bit of Texas with us. One of our guests' summertime favorites is Texas ribs—meaty beef ribs with a spicy dry rub, slow-cooked in the oven until they are tender, then finished on the grill with a generous mopping of sweet and smoky barbecue sauce. Forget about leftovers, though. I find that guests tuck into these ribs with abandon! YIELDS 6 SERVINGS

INGREDIENTS

8	pounds beef ribs
2	tablespoons garlic powder
2	tablespoons onion powder
1½	teaspoons coarse salt
1	teaspoon freshly ground black pepper
½	teaspoon cumin
½	teaspoon cayenne pepper
12	ounces beer

Sauce

1	tablespoon canola oil
½	cup onion, peeled and diced into ¼-inch pieces
5	large cloves garlic, peeled and minced
1½	cups ketchup
½	cup molasses
3	tablespoons balsamic vinegar
3	tablespoons brown sugar, packed
½	teaspoon Worchestershire sauce
½	teaspoon Liquid Smoke
¼-½	teaspoon Tabasco sauce

Preheat the oven to 275 degrees. In a small bowl, stir together the garlic powder, onion powder, salt, black pepper, cumin and cayenne pepper. Rub both sides of the ribs with the spice mixture, place them in a large roasting pan lined with foil, and pour the beer over the ribs. Cover the pan tightly with foil and braise the ribs in the oven for 1 ½ to 2 hours until the meat is knife tender and starts to pull back from the tips of the ribs.

While the ribs braise, preheat a medium saucepan over medium-low heat, add the oil, and swirl to coat the bottom of the pan. Add onion, sauté 2 minutes until it is soft, and add the garlic; cook 1 minute more. Stir in the ketchup, molasses, vinegar, brown sugar, Worchestershire, Liquid Smoke, and Tabasco. Reduce the heat to low and simmer 20 to 30 minutes, stirring occasionally.

Light the charcoal grill. When the coals are hot, rake them into two mounds on opposite sides of the grill to provide indirect heat. Transfer the ribs to the grill, reserving the braising liquid. Cook the ribs 20 to 30 minutes in the center of the grill, meat side down, moistening them with some of the braising liquid every 10 minutes. Baste the ribs with some of the molasses glaze and turn them over, meat side up. Cook the ribs 10 to 15 minutes more, basting frequently with the molasses glaze.

For gas grills, light one side of the grill. When it is hot, place the ribs on the opposite side of the grill and cook as directed above.

"...I like to bring a bit of Texas with us. One of our guests' summertime favorites is Texas ribs—meaty beef ribs with a spicy dry rub, slow-cooked in the oven until they are tender, then finished on the grill with a generous mopping of sweet and smoky barbecue sauce."

Kansas City Ribs with Sweet and Spicy Barbecue Sauce

Pork ribs—so meaty, juicy, and sizzling-hot off the grill, fragrant with a spicy dry rub and dripping with a sweet and spicy sauce—are the stuff great gatherings are made of. I've served these ribs several times since Randy and I have lived at *Swan's Nest,* and the eyes of my sweet neighbor Liz positively light up whenever she sees them. Without a doubt, these ribs are a summertime hit, perfect for Memorial Day, Father's Day, 4th of July, and Labor Day celebrations, or any time you feel like firing up the grill for lip-smacking pork ribs. YIELDS 6 TO 8 SERVINGS

INGREDIENTS

1	tablespoon garlic powder
1	tablespoon onion powder
1½	teaspoons Cajun seasoning
1	teaspoon kosher salt
½	teaspoon seasoned salt
½	teaspoon freshly ground black pepper
6	pounds pork loin back ribs
1½	cups apple cider

Sauce

1	tablespoon canola oil
½	cup onion, peeled and diced
3	cloves garlic, peeled and minced
1½	cups prepared chili sauce
⅓	cup ketchup
3	tablespoons dark brown sugar, packed
1	tablespoon cider vinegar
1	tablespoon molasses
1½	teaspoons Liquid Smoke
½	teaspoon Worcestershire sauce
¼	teaspoon cayenne pepper
	freshly ground black pepper, to taste

Preheat the oven to 275 degrees. In a small bowl, stir together garlic powder, onion powder, Cajun seasoning, kosher salt, seasoned salt, and black pepper. Rub the ribs with the spice mixture, transfer them to a large roasting pan, and pour the cider around the ribs. Cover the pan tightly with foil and braise the ribs 1½ hours until the meat is tender and begins to shrink back from the tips of the ribs.

Preheat a charcoal grill while making the sauce. Preheat a medium saucepan over medium-low heat, add oil, and swirl to coat the bottom of the pan. Add onion, sauté 2 minutes, stir in the garlic, and cook 1 minute more, stirring frequently. Add chili sauce, ketchup, brown sugar, vinegar, molasses, Liquid Smoke, Worcestershire, cayenne pepper, and black pepper, stirring well to mix. Reduce the heat to low and simmer 20 to 30 minutes, stirring occasionally.

When the coals are hot, rake them into two mounds on opposite sides of the grill to provide indirect heat. Transfer the ribs to the grill, reserving the cooking liquid. Cook the ribs 30 to 45 minutes, bone side down, in the center of the grill, mopping them with some of the reserved braising liquid every 10 minutes. Turn the ribs over and cook 15 minutes more, mopping them frequently with barbecue sauce.

Autumn Tables

I adore setting autumn-inspired tables for memorable gatherings. Translating nature's seasonal palette of deep russet, vivid gold, intense orange, and rich brown into a dreamy table setting my guests will love gives me particular pleasure when these hues take on a new richness in the flicker of candlelight. And when the colors are blended with textural elements and a bit of sparkle, the effect is dramatic and enchanting.

The autumn table pictured here was inspired by a copper and antique-gold remnant of fabric I purchased on sale in Dallas, and a set of elegant Czechoslovakian floral salad plates trimmed in gold I found in a Denver antique store. I folded and placed the heavy fabric down the center of the table to provide a textural foundation for the setting, and arranged a garland of silk autumn leaves over the fabric, accented with vases of fresh, autumn chrysanthemums and tiny pumpkins. Gold, puckered, silk-like placemats overlapped the edges of the fabric and were layered with large, matte-gold chargers and smaller copper chargers.

In an effort to add an element of rustic flavor to the table setting, I mixed casual, ironstone dinner plates with the rather formal chargers. The ironstone provided a delightful contrast to the antique china salad plates and complemented the matte-gold color found in the placemats and fabric table runner. In addition to the multiple layers of fabric, chargers, and dishware, I gave the table height and visual interest by pairing a variety of heavy, cut-crystal water goblets with delicate wine glasses rimmed in gold, and unembellished, generous sized, wine goblets. Tall, silver candlesticks holding copper-colored tapers and soft, ivory napkins, informally gathered into beaded napkin rings, completed the gracious setting.

Quail with White Beans

Each time I serve this dish, guests rave about it. It's one of those recipes that easily transforms from a cozy meal for four or six into a buffet dish that serves a crowd—just add extra quail and beans! The white beans gain their flavor from pan drippings after the meat is sautéed in the skillet, creating a savory "I can't get enough" taste sensation.

Of course, presentation is half the secret to any great recipe. Spoon the beans into the center of a platter and surround them with the quail. Garnish with fresh cilantro and you have a dish that goes from everyday simple to company worthy. YIELDS 4 TO 6 SERVINGS

INGREDIENTS

8	boneless quail breasts, rinsed and dried on paper towel
	kosher salt and freshly ground black pepper
1	tablespoon olive oil
⅔	cup sweet onion, peeled and finely chopped
½	cup green bell pepper, rinsed, seeded, and chopped
½	cup yellow bell pepper, rinsed, seeded, and chopped
2	large cloves garlic, peeled and minced
2	tablespoons jalapeño, rinsed, seeded and diced
2	15-ounce cans Great Northern beans, rinsed and drained
¼	cup chicken broth
1	small bunch fresh cilantro

Preheat a large skillet over medium heat, and season the meat on both sides with salt and pepper. When the skillet is hot, add oil and swirl to coat the bottom of the pan. Place the meat skin side down in the skillet and cook 3 to 4 minutes until the skin is golden brown. Turn the meat over and cook 3 minutes more, or until the meat is cooked through, but is still pink inside. Transfer it to a large platter and cover to keep it warm.

Add onion and bell pepper to the skillet and cook several minutes, stirring often to loosen brown bits from the bottom of the pan, until the peppers are crisp-tender. Add the garlic and jalapeño and cook 1 minute more. Stir in the beans and chicken broth, and cook just until the beans are heated through. Season with salt, pepper, and 1 tablespoon chopped fresh cilantro.

To serve, spoon the beans into the center of the platter and arrange the quail around the perimeter of the beans. Garnish the platter with a large sprig of cilantro.

Quail Breasts with Cocktail Grapefruit Sauce

Cocktail grapefruit is a cross between a Frua mandarin and a Pummelo, and is widely available from November through February. It's very juicy and sweet, with just a touch of tartness. In this recipe, the sweet fruit beautifully balances the fats of the quail, and adds a touch of easy elegance to this simple, but impressive dish. A final garnish of vibrant, red pomegranate seeds adds exquisite color and textural contrast. YIELDS 2 SERVINGS

INGREDIENTS

4	boneless breasts of quail, rinsed and dried on paper towel
1	cocktail grapefruit, zested, peeled, and sectioned, juice reserved
¾	teaspoon kosher salt
½	teaspoon ground cumin
½	teaspoon freshly ground coriander
¼	teaspoon pepper mélange
1	tablespoon olive oil
1	large clove garlic, peeled and finely chopped
¼	cup chicken broth
¼	cup reserved cocktail grapefruit juice
1	tablespoon pomegranate seeds, for garnish

Zest enough of the grapefruit to form 1 tablespoon medium-size zest and set it aside. Slice off both ends of the grapefruit and remove the remaining skin and outer pith with a sharp knife. To form whole segments of fruit, slice along each membrane with a paring knife. Place the segments on a small dish and set them aside.

Place a fine strainer over a glass measuring cup to collect any juices which have accumulated, and squeeze the juice from the fruit trimmings before discarding them.

In a small bowl, stir together salt, cumin, coriander, and pepper mélange. Sprinkle both sides of the meat generously with the seasoning mixture. Preheat a large skillet over medium heat, add oil, and swirl to coat the bottom of the pan. Place the meat skin side down in the skillet and cook 3 to 4 minutes until the skin is golden brown. Turn the meat over and cook 3 minutes more, or until the meat is cooked through, but is still pink inside. Transfer it to serving plates and cover to keep it warm.

Add the garlic to the pan and sauté 30 seconds until it is golden brown. Deglaze the pan with chicken broth and reserved cocktail grapefruit juice, scraping up any meat juices and brown bits from the bottom of the pan. Add reserved grapefruit sections and cook 1 to 2 minutes just until they are warmed through. Season the sauce with salt and pepper to taste.

To serve, arrange the grapefruit sections next to the quail, garnish with pomegranate seeds, and spoon some of the sauce around the meat.

Chicken Enchiladas with Mole Rojo

I love enchiladas—cheese, chicken, beef, or pork—they all satisfy my craving for Tex-Mex when served with a spicy red mole sauce. Here, I've streamlined the process of making the mole to obtain the same depth of flavor without all the fuss. The sauce is fabulous over enchiladas, but equally delicious mixed into shredded chicken or pork, and tucked into hot flour tortillas. YIELDS 4 SERVINGS

Mole

INGREDIENTS

2	dried New Mexico chiles
2	cups boiling water
1	tablespoon canola oil
¾	cup onion, peeled and chopped
2	large cloves garlic, peeled and chopped
1½	teaspoons cumin
1	teaspoon dried oregano
1	tablespoon cocoa powder
1	28-ounce can diced tomatoes
¾	teaspoon kosher salt
¼	teaspoon freshly ground black pepper
1	tablespoon reserved chile soaking liquid
1	slice dry wheat bread, cubed
1	4-ounce can diced green chiles
¼	cup chicken stock or chile soaking liquid

Place the chiles in a heatproof bowl, add the boiling water, and place a small plate over the chiles to keep them submerged. Soak 30 minutes or until they are soft.

Preheat a large saucepan over medium heat, add oil and swirl to coat the bottom of the pan. Add onion and sauté 3 to 4 minutes until it is soft, add the garlic, and sauté 1 minute. Season with oregano and cumin, stir, and add the cocoa. Stir quickly so the cocoa doesn't burn, quickly pour in the diced tomatoes, and stir well. Season the mixture with salt and pepper, and heat just until the mixture is warm.

Remove the softened chiles from the soaking liquid, reserving the liquid. Stem and seed one of the chiles, tear it into pieces, and place it in a blender. Add one-third of the warm tomato mixture and 1 tablespoon of the reserved soaking liquid, cover, and purée until it is smooth. Stem the remaining chile, tear it into pieces with some of its seeds, and transfer it to the blender with half of the remaining tomato mixture. Add chicken stock or ¼ cup of reserved soaking liquid, cover, and purée. Add the remaining tomato mixture, dry bread, and diced green chiles, and purée until the mole is smooth.

Return the mole to the saucepan, bring it to a simmer over medium heat, cover, and reduce the heat to low. Simmer 30 minutes, stirring occasionally. Add additional soaking liquid, 1 tablespoon at a time, if the mole appears too thick.

YIELDS 4 CUPS

Enchiladas

INGREDIENTS

8	8-inch whole wheat flour tortillas
2	cooked chicken breast halves, cut into ½-inch cubes
2	cups shredded cheddar cheese
2	cups shredded asadero cheese
½	cup onion, peeled and finely chopped
	Mole rojo
¾	cup sour cream, for garnish (optional)

Preheat the oven to 375 degrees. Spray a baking dish with non-stick cooking spray. Place a flour tortilla on a cutting board, add some of the chicken, cheddar and asadero cheeses, and onion. Roll up the tortilla and place it, seam side down, into the baking dish. Fill and roll the remaining tortillas. Spoon mole over the tortillas, cover, and bake 45 minutes or until the mole is bubbly and the enchiladas are hot. Garnish with sour cream, if desired.

Mango Sorbet

This refreshing sorbet is thick, rich, and brimming with mango flavor. It's a fabulous finale to a spring or summer backyard picnic, served in a dish or scooped into ice cream cones, and the pretty peach color is lovely as a delicate dessert for a ladies luncheon or Mother's Day celebration. You'll find this frosty sorbet is also a delightful dessert after a spicy Tex-Mex meal. YIELDS 4½ CUPS SORBET

Photo from Christy's Scrapbook

INGREDIENTS

1¼   cups water

1   cup sugar

3   large ripe mangos, rinsed and cubed

     juice of ½ fresh lime

Combine water and sugar in a small saucepan, stir well, and bring the mixture to a boil over medium heat, stirring frequently. Reduce the heat to low and simmer the sugar syrup 10 minutes. Remove it from the heat, stir in the lime juice, and set it aside to cool for 30 minutes.

Place the cubed mango in the bowl of a food processor and process until the fruit is puréed. Slowly add the cooled syrup and process until the purée is very smooth. Pour the mixture into an ice cream maker and freeze according to the manufacturer's instructions.

"*It's a fabulous finale to a spring or summer backyard picnic...*"

Apple Turnovers with Vanilla Bean Syrup

These puff pastry fruit turnovers, glistening with sparkling sugar, look divine served in a small pool of vanilla bean-flavored sugar syrup, but they are deceptively easy to make. For family gatherings or dinner with friends, this spiced apple dessert is make-ahead easy. YIELDS 4 SERVINGS

 TIP: At high altitude, bake the turnovers at 400 degrees for 25 minutes, then reduce the temperature to 350 degrees and bake them 5 to 10 minutes more until the apples are knife tender.

INGREDIENTS

1   sheet puff pastry, thawed
2   large Granny Smith or Golden Delicious apples, rinsed
⅓   cup granulated sugar
2   tablespoons brown sugar, packed
2   teaspoons flour
1¼ teaspoon Saigon cinnamon
¼   teaspoon freshly grated nutmeg
1   tablespoon freshly-squeezed lemon juice
1   egg
1   tablespoon water
1   tablespoon sparkling sugar

Adjust the oven rack to the center position and preheat the oven to 400 degrees. Roll out the puff pastry on a floured pastry cloth to a 12-by 12-inch square. Cut the pastry into four 6-inch squares and place them on a cookie sheet lined with parchment paper.

Peel, core, and slice the apples. In a medium bowl, gently stir them together with granulated sugar, brown sugar, flour, cinnamon, and nutmeg. Add lemon juice and stir gently to mix. Spoon the apple mixture into the center of each pastry, moisten the edges of the pasty with a brush dipped in water, and fold up and press opposite corners of the pastry together, to form a small packet. Press all edges together to seal the packet so juices do not escape during baking.

In a small bowl, whisk the egg and water together with a fork to form an egg wash. Brush some of the egg wash over the packets and sprinkle them with sparkling sugar. Bake 20 to 25 minutes until the pastry is brown and the apples are tender. Serve warm or at room temperature with vanilla bean syrup.

Vanilla Bean Syrup

This vanilla-flavored sugar syrup is a delightful change from the usual crème anglaise so often used to garnish fruit desserts. The syrup cooks in twenty minutes and may be made up to two hours ahead, but don't reheat it before serving, as the mixture will seize and turn solid. YIELDS ½ CUP SYRUP

INGREDIENTS

¾   cup water

½   cup granulated sugar

2   tablespoons light brown sugar

½   vanilla bean, split in half lengthwise

2   tablespoons unsalted butter

Combine the water, granulated sugar, brown sugar, vanilla bean, and butter in a medium saucepan. Bring the mixture to a boil, reduce the heat to medium, and cook on a low boil 20 minutes, stirring occasionally, until the syrup turns an amber color and coats the back of a spoon. Turn off the heat and set the syrup aside to keep warm. The syrup will remain a liquid for 2 to 3 hours. Do not reheat.

To serve, remove the vanilla bean, spoon a small amount of vanilla syrup in the center of each dessert plate, and place the turnover in the syrup.

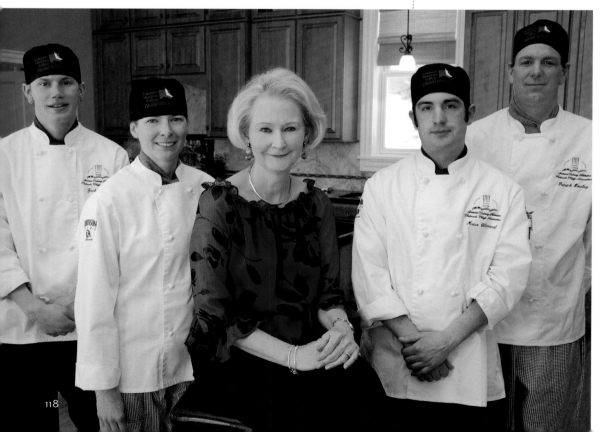

Christy with Culinary Student Assistants from Colorado Mountain College School of Culinary Arts, Breckenridge, Colorado Campus

In order L to R: Zach Brace, Jen Schilling, Christy, Mateo Villarreal & Patrick Howley

Cherry Streusel Cake

This cake is so pretty and absolutely delicious. It features a sweet streusel topping and cherry filling cushioned between layers of tender, almond-flavored cake. Perfect with coffee for a gathering of "the girls," it's just as lovely for teatime or as an easy dessert. The cake bakes beautifully both at sea level and high altitude with no adjustment of the ingredients. YIELDS 1 9- X 13-INCH CAKE

INGREDIENTS

½   cup unsalted butter, softened
4   ounces cream cheese, softened
1   cup sugar
2   eggs
1¾   cups flour
1   teaspoon baking powder
½   teaspoon salt
¼   teaspoon baking soda
½   cup milk
2   teaspoons vanilla
¾   teaspoon almond extract
1   21-ounce can cherry pie filling
1   cup flour
⅓   cup sugar
6   tablespoons cold unsalted butter, cut into
     ¼-inch cubes

Preheat the oven to 350 degrees. In a large bowl of an electric mixer, beat the ½ cup butter and cream cheese until they are blended, add sugar, and beat until the mixture is light. Add eggs, one at a time, mixing well after each addition.

In a small bowl, stir together flour, baking powder, salt, and baking soda. Add the flour mixture to the creamed mixture, alternately with the milk, beating well to form a thick batter. Stir in the vanilla and almond extract.

Spray a 9- by 13-inch cake pan with nonstick cooking spray. Spoon half the batter into the pan, tapping it lightly on the bottom to spread the batter evenly. Top the batter with the cherry pie filling, and spoon dollops of the remaining batter over the filling. Carefully spread the top layer of batter over the filling with an offset spatula.

In the bowl of a food processor, combine the remaining flour, sugar, and butter. Pulse until the mixture forms a dry meal, and sprinkle the crumb mixture over the cake. Bake 30 to 35 minutes, or until a cake tester comes out clean when inserted into the center of the cake.

Butternut Squash Pie

My Breckenridge friend Maggie said she likes this pie much better than pumpkin, and I can't think of a more delicious way to celebrate autumn's arrival. The pie has a lighter texture and slightly more delicate flavor than pumpkin pie, and while the flavor develops a bit more the second day, you may have trouble keeping it around long enough for that to happen! YIELDS 10 SERVINGS

INGREDIENTS

1	butternut squash, rinsed, about 1½ pounds
1½	cups flour
1	tablespoon sugar
¾	teaspoon salt
½	cup *cold* unsalted butter, cut into ½-inch cubes
5-6	tablespoons *ice* water
¾	cup sugar
1¼	teaspoons cinnamon
½	teaspoon ground ginger
½	teaspoon freshly grated nutmeg
¼	teaspoon ground cloves
⅛	teaspoon ground allspice
3	eggs
1	cup evaporated milk
1	cup heavy cream, whipped, for garnish
2	teaspoons confectioners' sugar, for garnish

Preheat the oven to 400 degrees. Slice the squash lengthwise, scoop out the seeds, and place it on a cookie sheet covered with parchment paper. Roast the squash 40 to 50 minutes, or until it is soft when pierced with a sharp knife. Cool, scoop out the pulp with a large spoon, and purée the pulp in a food processor or blender until it is smooth, about 1¼ cups.

For the pastry, place flour, 1 tablespoon sugar, and salt into the bowl of a food processor and pulse several times to mix. Add the butter and pulse until it is pea-size. Add ice water and process at low speed until the pastry is crumbly. If the mixture appears dry, add the remaining ice water and process just until the pastry comes together and forms a ball. Remove the pastry, wrap it in plastic wrap, and chill at least 30 minutes or until it is cold.

Preheat the oven to 425 degrees. In a large bowl, whisk together the puréed squash, remaining ¾ cup of sugar, cinnamon, ginger, nutmeg, cloves, and allspice. Add eggs and whisk until they are well blended. Slowly whisk in the evaporated milk.

On a floured pastry cloth or counter, roll out the pastry. Fold it in half and transfer it to a pie plate. Unfold the pastry, fit it into the pie plate, trim the pastry so it overhangs the edge by 1 inch, and flute the edge. Pour the filling into the pie shell and bake 15 minutes at 425 degrees. Reduce the heat to 350 degrees and bake 40 to 45 minutes more, or until the filling is set and a sharp knife inserted into the center of the pie comes out clean.

Remove the pie from the oven and set it aside to cool. In a large bowl, beat the heavy cream with confectioners' sugar until soft peaks form. Serve the pie with a dollop of Chantilly cream.

Banana and Pecan Foster Cake with Buttercream Frosting

During the twelve years Randy and I lived in Houston, Texas, we celebrated many anniversaries and other special occasions at Brennan's Restaurant, a sister property of the famous New Orleans establishment founded by Owen Edward Brennan. I remember gracious dining rooms, a friendly, professional staff that always seemed happy we were there and treated our young sons like fine little gentlemen, flutes of bubbly champagne with a plump, juicy strawberry floating within, bowls of steaming gumbo, perfectly cooked fish, fragrant yeast breads, and for dessert, Bananas Foster.

I've always loved Bananas Foster—a mixture of sautéed bananas, brown sugar, rum, banana liqueur, and ice cream first created in 1951 by Paul Blangé at Brennan's original New Orleans location. It brings back so many treasured memories, so you can understand why I am especially fond of this light, tender, and decadent banana cake that's garnished with buttercream frosting, glazed pecans, and "Foster" sauce drizzled down the outside of the cake. This special dessert is perfect for many memorable occasions. YIELDS 1 9-INCH TWO-LAYER CAKE

INGREDIENTS

⅔	cup milk
1	tablespoon cider vinegar
¾	cup unsalted butter, softened
1¼	cups granulated sugar
¼	cup dark brown sugar, packed
2	eggs
2¾	cups cake flour, sifted
1	teaspoon baking powder
1	teaspoon salt
½	teaspoon baking soda
1	teaspoon vanilla
2	ripe bananas, peeled and mashed

Preheat the oven to 350 degrees. Combine milk and vinegar; set it aside. In the large bowl of an electric mixer, cream butter, granulated sugar, and brown sugar until the mixture is light and fluffy, about 8 minutes. Add eggs, one at a time, beating well after each addition.

In a medium bowl, stir together flour, baking powder, salt, and baking soda. Gradually beat the flour mixture, alternately with the mashed banana and sour milk, into the creamed mixture to create a thick batter. Stir in vanilla.

Line two 9-inch round cake pans with parchment paper and spray the pans and paper with nonstick cooking spray with flour. Pour the cake batter evenly into the pans and bake 25 to 30 minutes, or until a tester inserted into the center of the cakes comes out clean. Cool the cakes 30 minutes, remove them from the pans, and place them on a wire rack to cool completely. Frost with buttercream frosting and garnish with Pecan Foster.

Buttercream Frosting

INGREDIENTS

6 tablespoons unsalted butter, softened

3¼ cups confectioners' sugar, sifted
    dash of salt

3 tablespoons milk

1 teaspoon vanilla

This frosting is very light and fluffy. After the frosting is mixed, I whip it with an electric mixer at high speed for several minutes to incorporate lots of air, which produces a light texture similar to whipped cream.

YIELDS FROSTING FOR A 2-LAYER NINE-INCH CAKE

In the large bowl of an electric mixer, cream butter and one-third of the confectioners' sugar, beating until the mixture is smooth. Gradually add the remaining confectioners' sugar and the salt, alternately with the milk, until the frosting is thick and fluffy. Stir in the vanilla. Beat the frosting at high speed 3 to 4 minutes more until it becomes very light and airy.

Place one cake layer on a cake plate and spread one-third of the frosting on top. Add the second layer and spread half of the remaining frosting on the sides of the cake. Top the cake with the remaining frosting and spread it evenly over the cake, sealing the edges. Decorate the cake with Pecan Foster.

"*I've always loved Bananas Foster—a mixture of sautéed bananas, brown sugar, rum, banana liqueur, and ice cream first created in 1951 by Paul Blangé at Brennan's original New Orleans location.*"

Pecan Foster

INGREDIENTS

1 tablespoon unsalted butter

¼ cup dark brown sugar, packed

1 tablespoon light corn syrup

2 teaspoons rum

½ cup pecan halves

Melt butter in a small saucepan over medium-low heat, add brown sugar, corn syrup, and rum, and stir until the mixture is smooth. Bring the syrup to a boil and cook 2 minutes, stirring constantly. Add pecans, reduce the heat to low, and cook 2 minutes, stirring constantly. Remove the pan from the heat and set it aside to cool.

When the syrup is cool, arrange the pecans along the top edge of the cake. Spoon the remaining syrup over the edge of the cake so it drips down the side.

CELEBRATING
MEMORABLE OCCASIONS

There are so many memorable occasions in our lives that deserve to be celebrated. Birthdays and anniversaries come immediately to mind, but a job promotion, high school or college graduation, a new home, or the arrival of special guests are equally of note. These milestone events deserve to be commemorated in a way that creates cherished memories to last a lifetime.

Years ago, my grandmother Henrietta flew to Dallas for a visit. It was her first time to see our Dallas home, and because she was well into her eighties, I knew her visit was one to be especially cherished and celebrated. I hosted an afternoon tea in my grandmother's honor, and all my friends attended. I sent out invitations, baked scones and tea cakes, decorated the front door, created floral centerpieces, and arranged beautiful tiered servers, silver trays, china cups and saucers, and a selection of teapots on the buffet table.

I knew as I prepared for the tea party that this would be an occasion my grandmother would describe many times to her friends back home in Pittsburgh, and it would be one I would cherish for the remainder of my life. What I did not expect was the number of friends who would to this day still speak fondly of that memorable afternoon. Without knowing, I had created an occasion to celebrate my dear Henrietta that meant almost as much to my friends as it did to my grandmother and me.

What is it that makes the celebration of an occasion memorable? I believe planning is essential, for rarely do events like these just "happen." I begin by creating a theme, for the theme dictates everything else—the invitations, colors, menu, table setting, accessories, and all the little special touches that will make the event unforgettable. In the case of a birthday, we all know children's parties revolve around cute decorations and activities to keep the kids busy and engaged. For an adult birthday celebration, my focus is on the invitation, menu, table setting, and simple decorative embellishments that engage my guests and make the honoree feel spoiled.

Invitations are a world unto themselves. If you walk into a stationery or party store, or search online, you'll find invitations in every style imaginable from the most casual and colorful to elegant and classic. One of my favorite, inexpensive options for birthday or dinner party invitations is printed cards produced for home computers, often found in office supply stores. I simply compose and type the text, print it out, tear the cards at the perforation, address, and mail.

Next comes the menu—something decadent, but not complex, for I learned a long time ago that one or two menu showstoppers is enough to leave a lasting impression. You'll find a fabulous duck recipe with a cherry-infused bourbon glaze in this section that's impressive, but incredibly quick and easy. Or beef tenderloin so tender it almost melts in the mouth, served with flaky, buttery puff pastry leaves that take only minutes to make. Pair that with my recipe for chopped salad trifle, attractively layered into individual glass bowls, and you have the beginnings of a memorable meal. Yes, you could serve a typical side salad, but imagine guests' delight when their salad appears in miniature glass vases usually reserved for flowers.

The tiniest departure from what is expected is often enough to create the "wow" factor so often associated with memorable occasions. That's why I like to surprise guests by serving an intermezzo course—a delicate scoop of homemade lemon sorbet to cleanse the palate, served in a martini glass between the soup or salad course and the entrée. This simple offering elicits smiles and awe, ensuring guests will remember and talk about the meal for a long time.

I've always said guests may not remember what they ate for dinner, but they always remember the dessert, so pull out all the stops when making dessert for a special occasion. For birthdays, red velvet cake, iced in light and airy seven minute frosting is a guaranteed showstopper. Add unexpected style and fun with tall, pencil-thin birthday candles, and your guests will ooh and aah. For other occasions, miniature desserts are all the rage, so I've included decadent, easy-to-make recipes for individual portions of chocolate mousse or white chocolate Bavarian with raspberry sauce.

Table settings take on added importance for special occasions. Depending on my theme, I like to use luxurious or fun fabrics, chargers that complement the theme or the color of the invitation, dinnerware layered to create visual impact, napkins folded creatively or inserted into napkin rings, place cards with guests names inscribed, floral accents in the center of the table or in front of each guest's place, lots and lots of candlelight at different heights, and overhead lighting dimmed to a romantic glimmer. For maximum impact, I combine votive candles or floating candles with tall candlesticks, sometimes using elegant tapers and other times substantial pillars. In my opinion, a host can rarely have too many candles, especially because every woman looks gorgeous in candlelight! The important thing to remember is that scented candles compete with the aromas and flavors of food, so always use unscented candles on the dining table.

Now, let's celebrate!

"The tiniest departure from what is expected is often enough to create the "wow" factor so often associated with memorable occasions."

Arranging Flowers

Fresh flowers add such magic to a home—color, fragrance, softness, contrast, seasonality, and graciousness. I have a collection of vases and containers in all shapes and sizes, from the smallest bud vase to provide a spot of color in a guest bath or a sign of welcome in a guest bedroom, to tall vases reserved for elaborate arrangements on the buffet or fireplace mantle.

At *Swan's Nest,* I also own a variety of swan-shaped containers that I dearly love. I created a multitude of swan centerpieces for a culinary industry luncheon I hosted a few years ago, much to the delight of my guests, and again more recently for an afternoon fundraising tea to benefit the Breckenridge Heritage Alliance. Arranging flowers in swan containers is like an unspoken nod to the rich heritage of our home and the gold baron who built it in 1898 and gave it its name. They also provide a touch of whimsy that keeps the floral arrangements from being too stuffy.

I purchased the swan vessels right after Randy and I bought *Swan's Nest,* before we had even begun restoring the house. I simply happened upon them one day, and knew if I didn't buy them immediately, I'd never find them again. Sure enough, during my next trip to the floral decorators' warehouse, there was not a swan vessel to be found.

What my assortment of swans illustrates is the importance of keeping an open mind when considering containers for flowers. Antique china casserole dishes with fluted edges and delicate handles, contemporary stemless wine glasses, teapots, and even tall candlesticks all make wonderful containers for floral arrangements. By thinking outside the box, I have the pleasure of enjoying a wide variety of floral arrangements, and that's half the fun.

Creating A Swan Floral Arrangement

SUPPLIES

Swan container
Floral oasis
Cutting board
Sharp knife to cut the floral oasis
Flower clippers
1 bunch roses
1 bunch alstromeria
Leather leaf fern

Measure the floral oasis against the swan container and cut it to fit with a sharp knife. Soak the oasis in a large bowl of cold water, adding additional water to the bowl as the water is absorbed. Do not submerge the oasis, as it will absorb enough water on its own.

Place the wet oasis into the swan and add a small amount of water to the container to a depth of 1 inch. Clip the stems of five roses 5 inches long. Insert two roses in the front corners of the oasis, one on each side of the swan's neck. Insert the third rose into the center of the oasis at the same height as the other roses, and the remaining two roses in the back corners of the oasis, one on each side of the swan's tail.

Clip the alstromeria stems five inches long, or 1 inch below the spot where the cluster comes together. Insert clusters of alstromeria among the roses to provide fullness. Divide the remaining alstromeria clusters into individual blossoms as needed to fill small spaces near the swan's neck and tail. Clip leather leaf ferns and insert their stems to cover any areas where the floral oasis is visible. Add water as needed to the swan container, dry the container with a towel, and place it on a protected surface so as not to damage furniture with moisture.

"*Fresh flowers add such magic to a home...*"

Butternut Squash Soup

This rich, flavorful vegetarian soup is delightful hot or cold when served as a first course. The addition of tart apple cider and a crisp apple add a nice flavor component to the soup. As a soup course for an elegant dinner, I like to serve it in rimmed soup bowls, but it's equally lovely in small ramekins or custard cups. If desired, add a dollop of crème fraîche or sour cream as a garnish.

YIELDS 6¼ CUPS OF SOUP

INGREDIENTS

1	tablespoon olive oil
1	cup sweet onion, peeled and chopped
½	cup carrot, rinsed, peeled, and chopped
½	cup celery, rinsed and chopped
4½	cups Butternut squash, rinsed, peeled, seeded, and cubed (about 1 ½ pounds)
1	Granny Smith or other tart apple, rinsed, peeled, cored & chopped
1	cup tart apple cider
4	cups vegetarian stock (I prefer KitchenBasics)
½	teaspoon kosher salt
½	teaspoon freshly grated nutmeg
⅛	teaspoon ground cardamom
⅛	teaspoon white pepper
½	teaspoon fresh thyme, chopped

In a large Dutch oven over medium heat, add oil, swirl to coat the bottom of the pot, and sauté onion, carrot, and celery 3 minutes or until the vegetables begin to soften. Add squash and apple, and sauté 5 minutes, stirring frequently, until they soften.

Deglaze the pan with apple cider and stir in the vegetable stock. Bring the mixture to a boil, reduce the heat to medium-low, and simmer 20 to 25 minutes, or until the squash is knife-tender. Add salt, nutmeg, cardamom, white pepper, and thyme, stir, and cook 5 minutes more. Remove it from the heat and purée the soup with an immersion blender, or cool it to lukewarm and purée the soup in batches in a blender. Caution: Hot liquids can build up pressure and explode in a blender, so always cool them before blending to avoid painful burns.

To serve, reheat the soup in a clean pot, or chill and serve cold.

Velvety Endive and Leek Potage

This creamy, velvety soup is a superb first course for a special meal. I like to serve it in the antique Limoges cream soup cups edged in gold that Randy gave me for our 25th wedding anniversary, but it would be equally lovely served in demi-tasse, small individual soufflé dishes, or china teacups.

The flavor of this soup is so delicately divine, it needs no adornment, but for an extra touch of decadence, add oysters or wild mushrooms during the final minutes of cooking, or garnish each soup cup with lump crabmeat or lobster. YIELDS 6 TO 8 FIRST-COURSE SERVINGS, ABOUT 3½ CUPS

CAUTION: Be certain to cool the soup base before puréeing in a blender, as hot liquids can build enough pressure to explode out of the blender and cause injury!

INGREDIENTS

1	tablespoon olive oil
1	large shallot, peeled and finely chopped
2	large cloves garlic, peeled and chopped
2	Belgian endive, rinsed and chopped
2	leeks, white and pale green parts, rinsed and finely chopped (about 1½ cups)
2½	cups chicken, vegetable, or seafood stock
½	cup heavy cream
½	teaspoon coarse sea salt
⅛	teaspoon white pepper
⅛	teaspoon cayenne pepper

In a large saucepan over medium heat, add the oil and swirl to coat the bottom of the pan. Add shallot and sauté 1 minute until it has softened. Stir in garlic, endive, and leek and sauté several minutes until they have begun to soften. Pour in chicken broth, bring the mixture to a boil, cover, and reduce the heat to medium-low. Simmer 10 to 15 minutes, or until the vegetables are soft. Remove the pan from the heat and set it aside to cool.

When the soup base is lukewarm, purée it in a blender until it is smooth and transfer the mixture to a large, clean saucepan. Stir in the cream and cook over medium-low heat until the soup is hot, stirring occasionally. Do not boil. Season with salt, white pepper, and cayenne, and stir well.

Baked Sherry Shrimp

I've been making this simple, elegant shrimp recipe for years, patterned after a similar dish we enjoyed in a Houston restaurant. As it bakes, the butter browns and develops a nutty flavor, which complements the sherry. For dinner parties, I bake and serve the shrimp in individual au gratin dishes, garnish each dish with a thin slice of lemon, and present it as a first course. I've also served the shrimp over rice as an entree. Either way, it's one of Randy's favorites. This recipe may be increased as needed for larger groups.

YIELDS 2 FIRST-COURSE SERVINGS

Often it's the simple things that leave a lasting impression on guests, such as these miniature crocks filled with butter, the tops smoothed with a knife, and garnished with dainty sprigs of fresh herbs.

INGREDIENTS

½	pound large, raw shrimp, rinsed, peeled and deveined, size 21-25
3	tablespoons unsalted butter
2	tablespoons sherry
1	tablespoon freshly squeezed lemon juice
¼	teaspoon paprika
1	lemon, rinsed and thinly sliced

Preheat the oven to 425 degrees. Divide the butter evenly between two heat-proof au gratin dishes and place them in the oven until the butter melts. Remove the dishes from the oven and transfer them to a heat proof surface. Add 1 tablespoon sherry and half the lemon juice to each dish and swirl to mix.

Divide the shrimp evenly between the two dishes, dip them into the butter mixture, and turn them over so both sides are coated in the mixture. Sprinkle the shrimp with paprika, cover the dishes with foil, and bake 10 to 12 minutes, or until the shrimp are pink and cooked through. Remove them from the oven, garnish with a slice of lemon, and serve.

Serving note: To protect tableware from the heat, place a doily or folded napkin under each au gratin dish prior to serving.

Mussels in White Wine

When the meal has to be impressive, but time is precious, this elegant but very simple first course is the answer. Mussels are steamed for just a few minutes in a savory wine and shallot broth, then served with a garnish of large caper berries in beautiful white bowls that show off the mussels' deep color. A loaf of rustic bread with a crusty exterior allows guests to sop up the last few drops of sweet, salty mussel and wine nectar.

I always check with my seafood department several days ahead to place my order, because mussels are alive and should be cooked the day they are purchased to ensure freshness. Store them in the refrigerator in a large bowl until just before preparation.

YIELDS 2 TO 3 MAIN DISH SERVINGS, OR 6 FIRST COURSE SERVINGS

INGREDIENTS

2	pounds fresh mussels
3	tablespoons unsalted butter
1	tablespoon olive oil
4	tablespoons shallot, peeled and finely chopped
2	large cloves garlic, peeled and finely chopped
¾	cup dry white wine
¼	teaspoon sea salt
	freshly ground black pepper
12	caper berries

Keep mussels chilled until shortly before cooking. Soak them in a bowl of cold water 15 minutes so they disgorge their sand, drain, and rinse. Remove any mussels with open or cracked shells and discard. To remove beards from the mussels, hold the mussel in one hand, grasp the beard with a towel, and pull it downward toward the shell's hinge.

Melt butter in a Dutch oven over medium-low heat, add the oil, and swirl the pan to mix. Sauté the shallot in the butter mixture 2 minutes, or until it is soft, add garlic, and sauté 1 minute more. Pour in the wine, add salt and pepper, and bring the mixture to a boil over medium-high heat. Add the mussels and caperberries, cover, reduce the heat to medium, and cook 4 to 6 minutes until all the shells have opened.

Spoon mussels into large bowls with some of the broth, garnish with caperberries, and serve with crusty bread to sop up the liquid.

Angel Hair Pasta with Oyster Mushrooms and Watercress

When it comes to pasta, I always believe simple is best. Pasta offers the ideal, neutral foundation to show off the flavors paired with it, and in this recipe, the peppery oyster mushrooms, nutty watercress, and salty Pamigiano Reggiano really shine through. The result is a medley of the pasta's "to-the-tooth" texture, combined with the mushrooms' pleasant chewiness and the crunch of the barely-sautéed watercress, all beautifully brought together in a delicate white wine sauce. YIELDS 4 SERVINGS

INGREDIENTS

½ pound angel hair pasta, cooked according to manufacturer's directions

1 cup reserved pasta cooking water

2 tablespoons unsalted butter

2 tablespoons olive oil

½ cup sweet onion, peeled and finely chopped

½ pound oyster mushrooms, cleaned and coarsely chopped

1½ cups watercress, rinsed and dried

3 large cloves garlic, peeled and finely chopped

½ cup dry white wine

¼ cup chicken or vegetable stock or broth
    kosher salt and freshly ground black pepper, to taste
    Parmigiano Reggiano, shaved, for garnish

Drain the cooked pasta, reserving 1 cup of the pasta cooking water, and set it aside to keep warm. In a large skillet over medium heat, melt butter, add the oil, and swirl to coat the bottom of the pan. Add onion and sauté 3 minutes or until it softens. Stir in oyster mushrooms, sauté 3 to 4 minutes until they are tender, and stir in the watercress and garlic. Cook 1 minute, stirring constantly.

Add wine, chicken stock, and ⅓ cup of the reserved pasta cooking water, bring the mixture to a boil, and add the pasta, tossing well to coat it with the sauce. Add additional pasta water, a little at a time, if the pasta appears dry. Season with salt and pepper, toss well, and transfer the pasta to a serving bowl. Garnish with shaved Parmigiano Reggiano.

Lemon Sorbet

For a significant event such as a milestone birthday or wedding anniversary, I love to pull out all the stops, embellish my table with layers of gorgeous fabrics, linens, china, and crystal, and serve dinner in courses to create a special dining experience.

This refreshing citrus sorbet is bursting with tart lemon flavor. I serve it in antique crystal champagne coupe stemware as an intermezzo to cleanse the palate between courses and provide an over-the-top dinner surprise for a truly memorable occasion.

YIELDS 12 INTERMEZZO SERVINGS

INGREDIENTS

1½   cups water
1¼   cups sugar
      zest of 1 large lemon
⅔   cup freshly squeezed lemon juice
      (about 4 small lemons)

Combine water, sugar, and lemon zest in a small saucepan, stir well, and bring the mixture to a boil over medium heat, stirring frequently. Reduce the heat to low and simmer the sugar syrup 10 minutes. Remove it from the heat, stir in the lemon juice, and set it aside to cool for 30 minutes.

Pour the mixture into an ice cream maker and freeze according to the manufacturer's instructions.

To serve, place a small scoop of sorbet into champagne coupes, martini glasses, or small bowls.

"This refreshing citrus sorbet is bursting with tart lemon flavor."

137

Fresh Mozzarella-Stuffed Roma Tomatoes with Basil Oil

I was intrigued several years ago when served a first course similar to this one at a tiny neighborhood restaurant in Dallas. I never forgot the impression that simple dish elicited, so I'm happy to share my own version with you. I like to plate this starter on small, white square appetizer dishes, with a small drizzle of basil oil around the base of the tomato. The vibrant contrast of colors and diminutive serving size is impressive—perfect for celebrating a memorable occasion.

During the summer, home-grown garden tomatoes from your garden or the farmers market are best, but if they're unavailable, look for Roma tomatoes that are fragrant and "give" with a little pressure from your thumb. YIELDS 6 TO 8 FIRST-COURSE SERVINGS

INGREDIENTS

6-8 Roma tomatoes
    sea salt and freshly ground black pepper
4 ounces fresh mozzarella cheese
1½ cups fresh basil leaves
⅔ cup extra virgin olive oil
    fresh basil leaves, for garnish

Slice the stem end from each tomato and discard. Cut a thin slice from the bottom of each tomato so it will stand upright on the plate. Peel the skin from the tomato with a very sharp vegetable peeler. Scoop out some of the pulp with a small melon baller or spoon and discard. Season the tomatoes with salt and pepper, fill the centers with mozzarella cheese, cover, and chill until just before serving.

Fill a large bowl with water and ice, and set it aside. Fill a large saucepan two-thirds full with water and bring it to a boil. Place the basil into the boiling water and blanch it 10 seconds just until it wilts. Remove the basil with a large slotted spoon and transfer it to the ice water to stop the cooking process. Remove the basil, squeeze it gently to remove as much water as possible, and roll it in paper towels to extract any remaining water.

Transfer the basil to a blender, add olive oil and a dash of salt, and blend 1 to 2 minutes on high speed until the oil is green with small flecks of whole basil. Transfer the basil oil to a squeeze bottle and set it aside until just before serving.

To serve, place a tomato on each plate, squeeze small dots of basil oil onto the plate in a decorative pattern, and garnish the plates with a small leaf of fresh basil.

Chopped Salad Trifle with Buttermilk Dressing and Applewood Smoked Bacon

I've always been intrigued with vases as creative containers for food, and glassware as vessels for flowers. It sounds backwards, but I can't resist the temptation to take a recipe that looks perfectly wonderful on a plate or in a bowl and find a way to serve it in individual glass containers. Hence, this chopped salad trifle.

When my mother-in-law Pat Rost Shilstone treated Randy and me to dinner out for my birthday, she ordered a chopped salad with a creamy dressing as a first course. Two days later, I came across a set of six square glass containers I had always used for votive candles or flowers, but suddenly I pictured that chopped salad, beautifully layered to reveal the textures and colors of crisp iceberg lettuce, spicy arugula, juicy red tomatoes, sweet basil, and tart red endive, with a creamy dressing flowing down the inside of the vase and crisp crumbles of applewood smoked bacon adding a final flourish. I'm happy to say the actual salad looks and tastes as divine as the one I envisioned. I first served it two weeks later for our 36th wedding anniversary dinner.

YIELDS 4 SERVINGS

INGREDIENTS

- 4   14-ounce square glass vases
- 1   red endive, rinsed and chopped
- 2   thick slices applewood smoked bacon, cooked until crisp
- 4½   cups iceberg lettuce, rinsed, spun dry, and coarsely chopped
- 1   cup arugula, rinsed, spun dry, and coarsely chopped
- 2   medium tomatoes, rinsed and chopped
- 2   tablespoons fresh basil, rinsed and julienned
      sea salt and freshly ground black pepper

Divide the endive equally into the bottom of each vase. Top with 2¼ cups of the chopped iceberg lettuce, arugula, tomatoes, basil, and the remaining iceberg lettuce, divided equally between each vase to form layers.

Just before serving, season the salads with salt and pepper, drizzle generously with buttermilk dressing, and garnish with crumbled bacon.

Buttermilk Dressing

A thick, creamy, tangy dressing that complements the sweet applewood smoked bacon, fresh tomatoes, and basil, as well as the slightly tart red endive in the chopped salad triffle. This dressing is so easy to make, you may wish to have it on hand for everyday salads, too! YIELDS ¾ CUP SALAD DRESSING

INGREDIENTS

1	clove garlic, peeled and chopped
½	cup mayonnaise
¼	cup lowfat buttermilk
½	teaspoon Dijon mustard (I prefer Maille)
¼	teaspoon kosher salt
¼	teaspoon freshly ground black pepper
¼	teaspoon onion powder

In a small bowl, crush the garlic with a fork. Add mayonnaise, buttermilk, mustard, salt, pepper, and onion powder, and whisk gently until the ingredients are well blended.
Cover and chill 1 hour or until ready to serve.

Sweet Potato and Apple Gratin

The secret to effortless entertaining is preparing as much of the menu in advance as possible. That's one of the reasons why I love this recipe. This gorgeous vegetable side dish for autumn and winter gatherings may be made early in the day, then baked shortly before serving. Layers of thinly sliced sweet potato and sweet-tart, orchard-fresh apples are baked in a light, creamy sauce with a touch of fragrant nutmeg and a whisper of white pepper. A panko crumb and parmesan cheese topping provide crisp texture and visual excitement. YIELDS 6 TO 8 SERVINGS

INGREDIENTS

4	large sweet potatoes, peeled and sliced into ¼-inch thickness
2	Granny Smith or other firm apples, peeled, cored, and thinly sliced
1	cup heavy cream
½	cup chicken or vegetable broth
½	teaspoon coarse salt
½	teaspoon freshly grated nutmeg
¼	teaspoon white pepper
½	cup grated Parmesan cheese
¾	cup panko crumbs

Preheat the oven to 350 degrees. Place a single layer of sweet potatoes in a large baking dish, overlapping the slices. Add a layer of sliced apple and top with the remaining sweet potatoes.

In a small bowl, stir together the heavy cream, chicken broth, salt, nutmeg, and white pepper. Pour the mixture over the potatoes and sprinkle with Parmesan cheese. Cover the casserole tightly with foil and bake 45 minutes. Uncover, sprinkle with panko crumbs, and bake 15 minutes more, or until the sweet potatoes and apples are tender when pierced with a sharp knife. Serve immediately.

Shitake Mushroom Risotto

Risotto is one of those recipes that are great for casual dinner parties. Friends always ask me if they can help in the kitchen, and most of my guests are in the kitchen anyway sipping wine and watching the action, so having a task such as stirring the risotto is a smart way to keep everyone entertained.

Risotto is an Italian dish made from Arborio rice, a thick grain that's high in starch and slower to absorb moisture than American long grain rice. And yet, when wine and hot stock are stirred into the Arborio rice a little at a time, the kernels become plump and tender with a creamy texture that is positively delectable. So round up family members or friends and put them in charge of stirring the risotto. It makes an elegant, memorable first course. YIELDS 6 SERVINGS

 TIP: At high altitude, the risotto will take 30 to 35 minutes to become al dente, and I used all 5 cups of the chicken stock.

INGREDIENTS

1½	cups shitake mushrooms, cleaned, stemmed, and chopped in ½ -inch cut
1	tablespoon olive oil
5	cups chicken stock or broth
¼	cup unsalted butter
½	cup sweet onion, peeled and finely chopped

1½	cups Arborio rice
½	cup dry white wine
	sea salt, to taste
⅛	teaspoon white pepper
	Parmigiano Reggiano, shaved, for garnish

> *"..having a task such as stirring the risotto is a smart way to keep everyone entertained.."*

In a small skillet over medium-low heat, add oil and swirl to coat the bottom of the pan. Add the mushrooms and sauté just until they are fragrant, about 1 minute. Remove them from the heat and set them aside.

In a medium saucepan, heat the stock over medium-high until it comes to a simmer, reduce the heat to low, and keep it warm. In a large saucepan over medium-low heat, melt the butter, add onion, and sauté 3 to 4 minutes until it is soft. Pour in the rice, stir until it is coated with butter, and cook it 2 to 3 minutes, stirring constantly. Pour in wine and cook until the wine evaporates, stirring constantly.

Add ½ cup hot stock, stirring the rice mixture until the liquid is almost absorbed. Continue adding hot stock, ½ cup at a time, stirring until the liquid is almost absorbed before adding additional stock. Cook 20 to 25 minutes, until most of the stock has been used and the rice is creamy and cooked al dente. During the final 3 minutes, stir in the mushrooms and season the risotto with salt and white pepper.

Serve the risotto immediately in large shallow bowls, and garnish with Parmigiano Reggiano.

Duck with Cherry-Infused Bourbon Glaze and Dried Figs

I was in college the first time I recall tasting duck. My folks took me to Cobb's Mill Inn in Weston, Connecticut—a picturesque restaurant that in its early days had been a grist mill. It closed a couple of years ago, which is such a shame, but I'm hopeful a new owner will breathe new life into the historic spot.

The mill was perched on the banks of a river, with a small dam that created a lovely little pond where ducks would swim and glide on the still water outside the restaurant's windows—providing entertainment for all the diners. They served a dish my folks called Duck Julie, though none of us are completely certain anymore whether that was the actual title on the menu. Duck Julie was prepared with an orange glaze, and I remember thinking it was divine. It was definitely one of my mother's favorites.

Here, I've paired a cherry-infused bourbon glaze and sweet, chewy dried figs with the crispy-skinned duck. The result is an impressive entrée that's a little bit different from the usual "company" fare, providing a bit of "wow" factor for special occasions. The subtle taste of cherries enhances the duck's natural flavor, while the mildly sweet, caramelized bourbon glaze is a nice complement to the figs. It's easy to make at home, looks gorgeous on the plate, and allows for partial cooking in advance—a definite bonus for a busy host.   YIELDS 4 SERVINGS

INGREDIENTS

4   12-ounce duck leg quarters
     coarse Mediterranean sea salt and
     freshly ground black pepper, to taste
¼   cup shallot, peeled and minced

⅔   cup cherry-infused bourbon whiskey
⅓   cup beef stock or broth
1   teaspoon dark brown sugar, packed
1   9-ounce package dried figs, stemmed and halved

Preheat the oven to 400 degrees. Rinse the duck and dry on paper towels and trim excess skin to the shape of the meat. Score the skin with a sharp knife to create a diamond pattern, taking care not to pierce the meat. Season both sides with salt and pepper.

Preheat a large skillet over medium heat. When it is hot, place the meat, skin side down, in the skillet and cook 4 to 5 minutes until the skin is brown and crisp, draining excess fat as needed. Turn it over and cook 4 minutes more to sear the meat. The meat may be prepared to this point, wrapped, and chilled overnight. Reserve the meat drippings and chill until shortly before making the sauce.

Transfer the meat to a roasting pan, drain the fat from the skillet, and set the skillet aside while the meat cooks in the oven. Roast the meat 30 to 35 minutes, or until it is pink inside and juices are clear when the meat is pieced with a fork. Remove it from the oven and cover to keep it warm.

While the meat rests, preheat the skillet over medium heat. When it is hot, add the shallot and sauté 1 minute, stirring constantly. Deglaze the pan with bourbon and beef stock, scraping up any brown bits on the bottom of the pan. Bring the sauce to a boil and cook until the liquid has reduced by half. Stir in the brown sugar and figs, and cook 2 minutes more, stirring frequently, until the sauce has thickened into a glaze. Spoon the glaze over the duck and garnish with the figs.

Herb Garden Roasted Pork Loin

As summer draws to an end and the first cool nights of autumn arrive, I crave the tantalizing aroma and sweet flavor of roasted pork. It's as if by placing a pork loin in the oven, dressed with garlic and fresh, fragrant herbs, and filling the house with a savory potpourri of tantalizing fragrances, I can hurry along autumn's arrival.

For special occasions, a beautiful roast of pork is impressive, but easy on the host. While the meat roasts slowly in the oven, I have time to make a first course soup or butternut squash pie, or to set the table in elegant shades of caramel, copper, gold, and moss green. **YIELDS 8 TO 10 SERVINGS**

INGREDIENTS

1	4-pound boneless pork loin roast
3	large cloves garlic, peeled and chopped
2	small cloves garlic, peeled and sliced
2	tablespoons fresh oregano, rinsed and chopped
2	tablespoons fresh parsley, rinsed and chopped
2	tablespoons fresh rosemary, rinsed and chopped
2	teaspoons fresh thyme, rinsed and chopped
1	tablespoon olive oil
	kosher salt and freshly ground black pepper

Preheat the oven to 400 degrees and tie the roast with string at 1-inch intervals so it roasts evenly. Make ½-inch deep slits along the fat side of the meat and insert a slice of garlic into each slit. Place the meat in a roasting pan, fat side up, and brush it lightly with oil. Season the meat with salt and pepper.

In a small bowl, stir together the chopped garlic, oregano, parsley, rosemary, and thyme. Pat the herb mixture along the entire top surface of the meat.

Roast the meat uncovered for 25 minutes, then reduce the temperature to 350 degrees and roast 60 minutes more, or until a meat thermometer registers 145 degrees when inserted into the center of the meat. Remove the pan from the oven, cover it loosely with foil, and allow the meat to rest 10 minutes before carving.

Fillet of Beef Tenderloin

Every once in a while, it's nice to pull out all the stops and bask in an air of pure decadence. Few entrées compare, much less surpass the opulence of a fillet of beef tenderloin. Its melt-in-your-mouth tenderness, flavor, and elegance on the plate can transform any gathering into a signature event.

Against the backdrop of a romantic wedding anniversary gathering with family and friends, the beef tenderloin holds center stage. For added romance and enjoyment, garnish the plates with savory puff pastry hearts. YIELDS 6 TO 8 SERVINGS

INGREDIENTS

1	3-pound fillet of beef tenderloin
1	tablespoon olive oil
1	teaspoon smoked sea salt flakes (I use Maldon)
	freshly ground pepper mélange
¼	teaspoon kosher salt
3	large cloves garlic, peeled and minced

Preheat the oven to 450 degrees. Tie the roast with string so it roasts evenly. Place it in a roasting pan, brush with olive oil, and season the meat with smoked sea salt, pepper mélange, and kosher salt. Sprinkle the top of the meat with minced garlic and roast it in the oven 40 minutes or until a meat thermometer registers 140 degrees for rare and 160 degrees for medium rare.

Remove the meat from the oven, cover it lightly with foil, and set it aside 10 minutes to rest. Carve the meat and serve with pan juices.

Savory Parmigiano Puff Pastry Leaves

Take your reputation as a home chef to the next level! Sometimes the smallest garnish can transform a special menu into an extraordinary dining experience. When the garnish is as easy and tasty as these flaky, buttery puff pastry leaves topped with Parmigiano-Reggiano, it makes being the perfect host almost effortless. Serve puff pastry leaves as a garnish to beef tenderloin or other roasted meats. **YIELDS 24 PUFF PASTRY LEAVES**

INGREDIENTS

1	package frozen prepared puff pastry sheets
1	egg
1	tablespoon water
¼	cup freshly grated Parmigiano-Reggiano cheese

"Sometimes the smallest garnish can transform a special menu into an extraordinary dining experience."

Remove one sheet of pastry from the package and return the remaining pastry to the freezer for another use. Wrap the pastry in plastic wrap so it doesn't dry out and thaw it at room temperature for 30 to 40 minutes until it unfolds easily.

Preheat the oven to 400 degrees. Unfold the pastry on a lightly floured pastry cloth or cutting board, flatten the folds with a floured rolling pin, and cut the pastry with a 2-inch leaf-shaped cookie cutter. Place the leaves on a cookie sheet lined with parchment paper.

In a small bowl, whisk the egg and water with a fork until they are well blended. Brush the top of each leaf with some of the egg wash and sprinkle with cheese. Bake 10 minutes, or until the leaves are puffed and golden brown. Serve as a garnish to meat dishes.

Beef Tenderloin Sandwiches with Roasted Garlic Mayonnaise

When leftover chilled beef tenderloin begs to be transformed into a decadent sandwich, all that's needed is thick slices of freshly-baked rustic bread and a generous slathering of roasted garlic mayonnaise. Tuck the sandwiches into a basket, grab a thermos of hot cider and some cookies, and you're all set for an autumn picnic or a couple hours of ice skating or sledding. YIELDS ENOUGH MAYONNAISE FOR 6 TO 8 SANDWICHES

INGREDIENTS

	leftover roasted fillet of beef tenderloin
1	loaf Pain de Campagne, whole wheat, or other rustic bread
4	large cloves garlic
1	teaspoon olive oil
½	cup prepared mayonnaise
1	teaspoon prepared horseradish
	freshly ground black pepper
1	small bunch watercress, rinsed, stems removed

At least two hours before serving, preheat the oven to 350 degrees. Place the garlic in a square of foil, drizzle it with oil, and close the foil tightly. Roast 30 to 35 minutes, or until the garlic is soft and fragrant. Remove it from the oven and set it aside to cool.

Squeeze the roasted garlic into a small mixing bowl and smash it with a fork until it is smooth. Stir in mayonnaise, horseradish, and black pepper until the mixture is well blended. Cover and chill 30 minutes to allow the flavors to develop.

Slice the bread into thick slices and spread them generously with some of the roasted garlic mayonnaise. Carve the beef thinly and place the meat on the bread to the desired thickness. Garnish with watercress, cover with the top slice of bread, and serve.

Overnight Guests

Have you ever stayed in a friend's or relative's home as an overnight guest and felt like you never wanted to leave? The host was no doubt dedicated to providing a tranquil experience that left you feeling pampered, spoiled, and refreshed.

During my college years, I had the privilege of staying overnight in Houston on several occasions with friends of my parents. Margie Bohn, sadly now gone, was an expert in creating a luxurious overnight guest experience, and I learned many lessons from her about how to become a gracious hostess. The canopy bed in her guest room was draped in gorgeous, lace-accented sheets and linens she ironed herself, flowers provided a cheerful welcome on the bedside table, an oversize, intricately carved bar of fragrant lavender soap awaited on soft towels in the bath, and the glass-topped, wrought iron breakfast table was set with beautiful tableware and warm-from-the-oven homemade cinnamon coffeecake. From the moment I arrived at the Bohn's home to the moment I left, I was wrapped in an aura of welcome and luxury that stayed with me long after I departed.

I take great pride in providing a similar experience for our overnight guests. One day, years after our son Bob had left for college, I was home in Dallas on business when it struck me that his room—now our guest accommodations—left a lot to be desired. By day, I attended meetings and filmed episodes for the Texas cooking show I hosted, but by night, I purchased a dramatic hue of gold paint for the walls, a new queen-size bed and carved headboard I found on a spectacular sale, and a beautiful quilt and matching bed linens. I pulled as much furniture as I could manage out of the room, covered the rest with plastic, and spent several late nights painting the walls. When it was time to move everything back into the room and begin its transformation into a comfortable guest room, I fondly recalled cherished memories of the room Margie Bohn prepared for my visits.

Swan's Nest

"...it's the small touches that put guests at ease and signify loving care."

Likewise at *Swan's Nest,* before the lathe and plaster walls—full of holes and decay—had been removed in preparation for restoration, I was already envisioning the special guest room I would create for my sisters and other guests. It would be a room fit for royalty—a place of un-paralleled relaxation and pampering. I selected the north bedroom as our very special guest room, the one Randy and I deduced had belonged to Ben Revett after we found several of his possessions inside the walls.

It was fun watching the room take shape over a period of many months, and while I'm not sure anyone else could envision how beautiful the room would one day be, I always knew it was going to be gorgeous. A fabulous wrap-around fiery cherry bed that everyone assumes is an antique, an oversized matching side table, a luxurious comforter of blue and gold with mounds of downy pillows, an Oriental rug that keeps toes warm first thing in the morning, a window seat built into an alcove overlooking the majesty of 12,000 foot mountain peaks, two roomy closets, 19th century woodwork restored to its original beauty, a crystal chande-lier Ben Revett would have loved, and giant double-hung windows with a view of the forest behind our house. The room is a retreat that lives up to what I envisioned.

Creating an overnight experience guests will remember fondly isn't about having the perfect guest room. Instead, it's the small touches that put guests at ease and signify loving care. A modest bed behind a screen in the corner of a room may be every bit as luscious when embellished with pretty linens, a small table with a good reading lamp, a selection of interesting reading material, and a small vase of flowers. A breakfast tray or mid-afternoon tea tray

delivered to the room by the host transforms any accom-modations into a suite at the Waldorf-Astoria. Thick, absorbent towels, fragrant soap, and a few flowers in the bath invite guests to linger and relax. A note of welcome on the bed and a tray with a small water pitcher, glasses, and a few pieces of fruit are simple but gracious touches that convey to guests how happy you are to host them.

Orange Scones

Overnight guests to *Swan's Nest* or our home in Dallas can always count on being spoiled. Surprising them with something fragrant from the oven, like these scones, is a nice way to wake up the first morning. Sweet, tender, and full of zesty orange flavor and tangy cranberries, then drizzled with frosting, this is a treat they won't mind getting up for in the morning. These scones are also scrumptious with a pot of hot tea on a chilly afternoon or after a summer hike through the mountains. YIELDS 8 TO 10 SCONES

INGREDIENTS

2 cups flour

¼ cup sugar

2 teaspoons baking powder

¾ teaspoon salt

½ cup fresh or frozen cranberries

½ cup cold unsalted butter, cut into ½-inch pieces

2 eggs, divided use

1 orange, zested

3 tablespoons freshly squeezed orange juice

3-4 tablespoons half-and-half

1 tablespoon sparkling or granulated sugar, for garnish

2 cups confectioners' sugar, sifted, for glaze

2-3 tablespoons milk, for glaze

Preheat the oven to 375 degrees. In a large bowl, stir together flour, sugar, baking powder, and salt until they are well blended.

In a small food processor, pulse the cranberries until they are coarsely chopped and add them to the flour mixture.

In a small bowl, whip 1 egg with a fork and stir in the orange zest and juice. Pour the egg mixture into the flour mixture, add 3 tablespoons of the half-and-half, and stir just until the mixture comes together. If the dough is too dry, stir in the remaining half-and-half. Turn the dough out onto a floured pastry cloth or counter and knead it several times until the dough is smooth.

Roll out the dough into a 13-inch by 4½-inch rectangle with a ⅝-thickness, tapping the edges with a metal pastry scraper to keep them even. Cut the dough into triangles with a sharp knife and transfer the scones to a lightly greased cookie sheet.

In a small bowl, whip the remaining egg with 1 tablespoon water to form an egg wash. Brush the egg wash over the tops of the scones and sprinkle them with sparkling sugar. Bake 15 to 17 minutes, or until the tops are golden brown. Remove them from the oven and transfer them to a wire rack to cool.

When they are cool, whisk together the confectioners' sugar and milk in a medium bowl to form a thick glaze. Drizzle the glaze over the scones in a zigzag pattern and set them aside until the glaze has dried.

Key Lime Pie

Key lime pie is, hands down, Randy's favorite dessert. Whenever we dine out, especially if we're vacationing in Florida, I know without asking what Randy will order for dessert.

Randy's infatuation with key lime pie goes back many years. I realized it when we were vacationing on Padre Island in southern Texas, just weeks before our son Timothy was born. Our first night on Padre, we took the bridge back to the mainland and dined in a small restaurant near the Port Isabel Lighthouse. I don't recall what we ate for dinner, but I do remember the key lime pie. It was light, sweet, and tangy, with a graham cracker crust and a swirl of whipped cream. We asked about the pie and were told a local woman baked all their key lime pies. While we never met the baker, Randy and I were so impressed, we dined there again two nights later. That woman's pies created a lasting memory. I like to think she would approve of my version. Randy loves it! YIELDS 8 SERVINGS

INGREDIENTS

1¼   cups graham cracker crumbs, about 8 whole crackers

2   tablespoons sugar

1½   teaspoons fresh key lime zest

¼   cup unsalted butter, melted

4   egg yolks

1   14-ounce can sweetened condensed milk

½   cup key lime juice

1   cup heavy cream, for garnish, if desired

1   tablespoon confectioners' sugar

Preheat the oven to 325 degrees. Process the graham cracker crumbs in a food processor or blender to yield 1¼ cups crumbs.

In a medium bowl, stir together the cracker crumbs, sugar, key lime zest, and melted butter until the crumbs are moist. Pour the mixture into a 9-inch pie plate and press it with fingertips into the bottom and up the sides of the pie plate. Bake 10 minutes and set it aside to cool completely.

Raise the heat to 350 degrees. In a large bowl, whisk egg yolks, sweetened condensed milk, and key lime juice together until the mixture begins to thicken. Pour the filling into the pie crust and bake 15 minutes. Remove it from the oven, set it aside to cool, and chill the pie several hours or overnight. Whip heavy cream and confectioners' sugar together until it forms soft peaks. To serve, garnish each slice with a swirl of sweetened whipped cream, if desired.

Blueberry Amaretti Fool

Photo from Christy's Scrapbook

For a special occasion such as Mother's Day, a lady's birthday, bridal shower, or a memorable dinner party, this pretty-as-a-picture layered dessert is one you and your guests will remember fondly. Sweet blueberry compote is gently folded into a whipped cream-Greek yogurt mixture to reveal vibrant streaks of blue and white, then layered with crushed Amaretti cookies and fresh berries into stately wine glasses. It's light, refreshing, and divine! Best of all, this dessert may be prepared one day ahead.

If you use frozen blueberries for the compote, for optimum flavor I suggest fresh berries that you have tucked away into your freezer. To freeze fresh blueberries for later use, rinse them well, turn them out onto a towel lined with paper towels to avoid stains, and dry them gently. Transfer the berries to a cookie sheet, place it in the freezer until the berries are frozen, and gently scoop them into plastic freezer bags for storage. The frozen blueberries will keep for several months. YIELDS 6 SERVINGS

INGREDIENTS

1½	cups fresh or frozen blueberries
⅓	cup granulated sugar
1	tablespoon water
2	teaspoons freshly squeezed lemon juice
1½	cups heavy cream
¾	cup (6 ounces) nonfat plain Greek yogurt
1	tablespoon confectioners' sugar
1	teaspoon vanilla
15	Amaretti cookies, coarsely crumbled
¾	cup fresh blueberries, for garnish

"*Sweet blueberry compote is gently folded into a whipped cream-Greek yogurt mixture to reveal vibrant streaks of blue and white, then layered with crushed Amaretti cookies and fresh berries into stately wine glasses.*"

Early in the day or a day in advance, in a medium saucepan over medium-high heat, stir together 1½ cups blueberries, granulated sugar, water, and lemon juice. Bring the mixture to a boil, reduce the heat to medium, and simmer 10 minutes, stirring occasionally, until the berries soften and the juices begin to thicken. During the final 2 minutes of cooking, reduce the heat to low and crush the berries gently with the back of a spoon. Remove it from the heat, pour it into a bowl, and set it aside to cool. Cover and chill the blueberry compote until it is cold.

In a large bowl of an electric mixer, beat heavy cream just until it begins to thicken. Add the yogurt, confectioners' sugar, and vanilla, and beat until soft peaks form. Transfer half of the whipped cream mixture to another bowl and gently fold in the chilled blueberry compote just until streaks of blueberry and whipped cream show.

To assemble, spoon a small amount of the whipped cream mixture into the bottom of 6 wine glasses, sprinkle with crushed Amaretti cookies, and top with some of the blueberry cream mixture. Arrange 5 fresh blueberries on top of the blueberry cream mixture so they show against the sides of the glass. Sprinkle the center with crushed cookies. Top with another layer of the whipped cream mixture, more fresh berries around the sides of the glass, crushed cookies, and a final layer of the blueberry cream mixture. Garnish the center of the glass with a dollop of whipped cream mixture, a blueberry on top, and a sprinkle of crushed cookies. Chill the Fool until ready to serve.

Chocolate Mousse

When Randy and I moved to Paris, France, we hired a sitter for the boys one evening and dined in a restaurant called Les Trois Mouton, The Three Lambs. I don't remember what my dinner was that night, but I could never forget the dessert—mousse au chocolat.

Two ladies were seated at a nearby table, and one of them had her little white dog tucked under the table by her feet—my first encounter with the love the French have for their dogs. The ladies were well dressed and appeared just as interested in us as we were in them. Randy and I were young, had only been in Paris a couple of weeks, and it was our first night out on the town without our little boys. I guess it showed.

When the ladies had finished their meal, the waiter brought them a large, white crock full of chocolate mousse. I had never seen anything like it! The ladies served themselves from that seemingly bottomless crock, chatting and laughing like young girls, so there was no question what Randy and I were going to order for dessert! The waiter brought dessert menus and we ordered mousse au chocolat with great anticipation—only when he brought our order, it wasn't in a crock. Randy and I were heartbroken, but without a moment's hesitation, one of the ladies summoned the waiter, spoke a few words, and the waiter quickly replaced our dessert with a gleaming white crock filled to the brim with decadent mousse au chocolat. In my still rather limited French, I expressed our sincere thanks to those lovely ladies who transformed our first romantic dinner in Paris into a deliciously unforgettable experience. YIELDS 12 3-OUNCE SERVINGS

INGREDIENTS

2¼	cups heavy cream		dash of salt
1	vanilla bean	3	tablespoons sugar
5	egg yolks	8	ounces bittersweet chocolate, 60% cacao

Split the vanilla bean in half lengthwise with the tip of a sharp knife, place it in a medium saucepan, and add 1 cup of the heavy cream. Bring the cream to a boil over medium heat, reduce the heat to low, and simmer 2 minutes. Turn off the heat and set it aside to keep warm so the vanilla bean can fully infuse the cream.

In a medium bowl, beat egg yolks with salt, and gradually add the sugar, beating until the mixture is thick and pale. Strain the hot cream into a clean saucepan, then whisk half the cream into the egg mixture. Pour the tempered egg mixture back into the saucepan and cook over medium heat, whisking constantly, until the custard thickens and just

comes to a boil. Set is aside until it is lukewarm.

Chop the chocolate, place it in a medium-size heatproof bowl, and microwave at 50 percent power 3 to 4 minutes, or until it is almost melted. Stir until the chocolate is fully melted and quickly whisk in the warm custard until the mixture is well blended.

In a large bowl, beat the remaining heavy cream until soft peaks form. Gently fold the whipped cream into the chocolate mixture until it is completely combined. Spoon the chocolate mousse into three-ounce bowls, demi-tasse cups, or small ramekins, and chill at least one hour. Cover and chill overnight, if desired.

Raspberry Coulis and White Chocolate Bavarian

Randy and I hosted an elegant dessert buffet party to celebrate the engagement of our son Bob to his sweetheart, Erin. I pulled out all the stops and baked for a week so this would be a celebration the young couple would always cherish. The table and dining room buffet were overflowing with one sweet delicacy after another, and our sixty guests were enchanted by the selection and presentation. One dessert that elicited the most oohs and aahs was this raspberry coulis and white chocolate Bavarian—a two-layered, mini-dessert of sweet and tangy raspberry coulis topped with light-as-air white chocolate custard, presented in shot glasses and displayed on a tiered server. Simply sublime! YIELDS 26 TO 28 MINI-DESSERTS

Raspberry Coulis

INGREDIENTS

6	ounces fresh or frozen raspberries, thawed
1½	tablespoons sugar
½	teaspoon freshly squeezed lemon juice

Place the raspberries in a blender, add sugar and lemon juice, and purée until it is smooth. Transfer the mixture to a fine sieve set over a bowl and, using the back of a spoon, push the purée through the sieve. Discard the seeds, cover the coulis, and chill.

White Chocolate Bavarian

INGREDIENTS

2	tablespoons cold water
1	tablespoon unflavored gelatin
2½	cups milk
1	cup heavy cream
4	eggs
⅔	cup sugar
4	ounces white chocolate, coarsely chopped
1½	teaspoons vanilla
¾	cup heavy cream, whipped to soft peaks

I find it easier to prevent the raspberry coulis from seeping up the outside of the custard filling if after pouring a teaspoon of coulis into the bottom of each glass, I spoon just enough Bavarian on top of the coulis to seal it in; then chill for 10 minutes. Once I spoon the remainder of the Bavarian into the glasses, the red coulis stays at the bottom without rising through the custard.

In a small bowl, sprinkle gelatin over the water and set it aside until the gelatin has softened. In a large saucepan, stir together the milk and 1 cup of heavy cream.

Separate the egg yolks from the whites, reserving the whites for another use. In a medium bowl, whip the egg yolks with an electric mixer until they begin to thicken. Gradually add sugar and beat until the yolks are pale and very thick. Gradually whisk in half of the hot milk mixture to temper the eggs, then pour the egg mixture into the sauce-pan. Cook over medium heat, whisking constantly, until the custard thickens and just comes to a boil.

Place the chopped white chocolate in a large, heat-proof bowl. Pour in the hot custard, vanilla, and softened gelatin, and stir to melt the chocolate. Chill the custard 45 to 60 minutes, or until it has thickened to the consistency of raw egg whites. Gently fold in the whipped heavy cream.

To assemble, spoon 1 teaspoon raspberry coulis into the bottom of the shot glasses, taking care not to drip coulis down the sides of the glasses. Carefully spoon the custard mixture into each shot glass, dividing it equally among all of the glasses. Cover and chill until ready to serve.

Cake Decorating

I baked and decorated this Lemon Chiffon Celebration Demi-Cake for a dear friend's birthday, but it would be equally appropriate as a celebration of Mother's Day or the first day of Spring. I turned to Mother Nature for inspiration when decorating this cake. Here, bright yellow, daisy-like chrysanthemums provide the color scheme, but the first time I made the cake, my pansies were growing by leaps and bounds in my Dallas garden, so I topped the cake in purple, blue, and white pansies. It was gorgeous!

To decorate the cake as I've done here, select a color scheme based on flowers that are readily available either in the store or in your garden. Be certain the flowers have not been sprayed with chemicals. Ice the two-layer cake with Whipped Buttercream Frosting and tint one-third of the remaining frosting with yellow food coloring. Transfer the tinted frosting to a cake decorator bag fitted with a small plain tip (Ateco #3 or Wilton #3). Hold the decorator bag directly over the spot you wish to form the dot, and pipe small dots of yellow frosting, using equal spacing around the entire side of the cake.

Transfer the remaining untinted buttercream frosting to another decorator bag fitted with a large star tip (Ateco #843 or Wilton #21). Hold the decorator bag at a 45 degree angle next to the top edge of the cake and touch the top surface of the cake lightly with the tip. Squeeze the bag using steady pressure, move the tip up and toward you, then back down to the cake surface. Stop the pressure and pull the tip away to form a shell. Place the tip at the end of the first shell and repeat the process around the entire rim of the cake.

Select flowers that are similar in size. Using sharp scissors, cut the flowers, leaving a ¾-inch stem. Insert the flowers into the cake just inside the shell border, overlapping the edges of the flowers somewhat to completely cover the top of the cake. Insert one or two flowers in the center of the cake and place it in the refrigerator until just before serving.

Lemon Chiffon Celebration Demi-Cake

When a large cake is too much, this two-layer miniature version provides big flavor in a diminutive 4-inch size, and proves the adage that "big things come in little packages." I created this light-as-a feather lemon cake for my friend Dyan to celebrate her birthday on a beautiful early-spring day. It's perfect for birthdays, Mother's Day, showers, afternoon tea, and other special occasions. **YIELDS 4 TO 6 SERVINGS**

INGREDIENTS

4	tablespoons unsalted butter, softened
½	cup plus 2 tablespoons sugar
1	teaspoon lemon zest
1	egg yolk
1	teaspoon freshly squeezed lemon juice
½	teaspoon vanilla
¾	cup flour
½	teaspoon baking powder
¼	teaspoon salt
⅓	cup milk
1	egg white
⅛	teaspoon cream of tartar

Preheat the oven to 350 degrees. In the large bowl of an electric mixer, cream butter, sugar, and lemon zest until the mixture is light and fluffy, about 8 minutes. Add egg yolk, beat well, and stir in the lemon juice and vanilla.

In a large bowl, stir together flour, baking powder, and salt. Gradually beat the flour mixture, alternately with the milk, into the creamed mixture to create a thick batter.

In a medium bowl, whip the egg white with an electric mixer until it foams, add the cream of tartar, and whip until soft peaks form. Gently fold the egg white into the cake batter until it is well blended.

Grease two 4-inch round cake pans and line them with parchment paper. Spoon the batter into the pan and bake 25 to 30 minutes, or until a cake tester comes out clean when inserted into the middle. Cool the cakes on a wire rack 20 minutes, remove them from the pans, and cool them completely. Frost with Whipped Buttercream Frosting.

Whipped Buttercream Frosting

Heavy cream gives this sweet, fluffy frosting its very light texture. The recipe makes enough frosting for a two-layer 4-inch diameter cake, plus a little extra for decorating.

YIELDS FROSTING FOR A 2-LAYER FOUR-INCH CAKE

Photo from Christy's Scrapbook

INGREDIENTS

5 tablespoons unsalted butter, softened

3 cups confectioners' sugar, sifted

4-5 tablespoons heavy cream
  dash of salt

½ teaspoon vanilla

In the large bowl of an electric mixer, cream butter and one-third of the confectioners' sugar, beating until the mixture is smooth. Gradually add the remaining confectioners' sugar and the salt, alternately with the cream, until the frosting is thick and fluffy. Stir in the vanilla.

Red Velvet Cake

I remember seeing my first Red Velvet Cake when I was in sixth grade. I was eating lunch with my friends in a school cafeteria in Pitcairn, Pennsylvania, when a girl in the next row carefully unwrapped a slice of bright red cake her mother had sealed in foil. It was a single layer with snow-white frosting, and I thought it was the prettiest cake I had ever seen. I could only imagine how it tasted, but I was certain it was divine.

Years later, I would learn that Red Velvet Cake is a traditional Southern dessert, often topped with cream cheese frosting. My version features an extra dash of cocoa in the batter to provide added flavor and a cloud of fluffy frosting. This is a beautiful, memorable cake to celebrate any special occasion. YIELDS 1 9-INCH TWO-LAYER CAKE

 TIP: The measurements are so different for this cake to bake successfully at high altitude, I have completely rewritten it with the high-altitude measurements and instructions on the following pages.

INGREDIENTS

⅔	cup milk
2	teaspoons cider vinegar
¾	cup unsalted butter, softened
1¾	cups sugar
2	eggs, at room temperature
1½	tablespoons red food coloring
1½	teaspoons vanilla
2¾	cups cake flour, sifted
2½	tablespoons cocoa, sifted
¾	teaspoon baking powder
¾	teaspoon salt
¼	teaspoon baking soda

Preheat the oven to 350 degrees. Add vinegar to the milk, stir, and set it aside to sour.

In the large bowl of an electric mixer, cream butter and sugar until the mixture is light, about 8 minutes. Add eggs, one at a time, beating after each addition. Add food coloring and vanilla, beating until they are well blended.

In a medium bowl, stir together cake flour, cocoa, baking powder, salt, and baking soda. Gradually beat the flour mixture, alternately with sour milk, into the creamed mixture. The batter will be light and fluffy.

Line two 9-inch round cake pans with parchment paper, then spray the pans and the paper with nonstick cooking spray with flour. Pour the cake batter evenly into the pans, and bake 28 to 30 minutes, or until a tester inserted into the center of the cakes comes out clean. Cool the cakes on a wire rack 30 minutes, remove them from the pans, and cool completely. Frost the cakes with Seven-Minute Frosting.

High-Altitude Red Velvet Cake

The measurements are so different for the Red Velvet Cake to bake successfully at high altitude, I have completely rewritten it with measurements that work well in my Breckenridge, Colorado, kitchen at 9,300 ft elevation. Cakes can rise quickly and fall in the center when baked at higher elevations, due to the lower air pressure, so I've adjusted the proportions of flour, sugar, and leavening so your cake will look and taste as beautiful as the one pictured on the previous page. YIELDS 1 9-INCH TWO-LAYER CAKE

INGREDIENTS

⅔	cup plus 1 tablespoon milk
1	teaspoon cider vinegar
¾	cup unsalted butter, softened
1½	cups sugar
2	eggs, at room temperature
1½	tablespoons red food coloring
3	teaspoons vanilla
1	cup cake flour, sifted
1¾	cups all purpose flour
2½	tablespoons cocoa, sifted
½	teaspoon baking powder
¾	teaspoon salt
¼	teaspoon baking soda

Adjust the oven racks to the middle of the oven and preheat it to 350 degrees. Add vinegar to the milk, stir, and set it aside to sour.

In the large bowl of an electric mixer, cream butter and sugar until the mixture is light, about 8 minutes. Add eggs, one at a time, beating after each addition. Add food coloring and vanilla, beating until they are well blended.

In a medium bowl, stir together cake flour, all purpose flour, cocoa, baking powder, salt, and baking soda. Gradually beat the flour mixture, alternately with sour milk, into the creamed mixture. The batter will be light and fluffy.

Line two 9-inch round cake pans with parchment paper, then spray the pans and the paper with nonstick cooking spray with flour. Pour the cake batter evenly into the pans, and bake 28 to 30 minutes, or until a tester inserted into the center of the cakes comes out clean. Cool the cakes on a wire rack 30 minutes, remove them from the pans, and cool completely. Frost the cakes with Seven-Minute Frosting.

Seven-Minute Frosting

This frosting is fluffy, ultra-white, and pleasantly sweet. It looks gorgeous on Red Velvet and dark chocolate cakes, and holds up well for several days when the cake is chilled between servings. YIELDS FROSTING FOR A 2-LAYER CAKE

INGREDIENTS

2   egg whites, at room temperature
⅓   cup water
¼   teaspoon cream of tartar
1¼   cups granulated sugar
½   teaspoon vanilla

Bring a saucepan of water to a simmer. Place egg whites and ⅓ cup water in a heat-proof bowl and beat with an electric mixer until the mixture begins to foam. Add cream of tartar and beat 1 minute until the egg whites start to thicken. Place the bowl over simmering water, but do not allow the bowl to touch the water. Continue beating until the egg whites double in volume.

Gradually add sugar, beating until the frosting is thick, glossy, and holds its shape, about 5 minutes. Remove it from the heat and stir in the vanilla. Frost the cake and chill until ready to serve.

High Altitude Seven-Minute Frosting

For high-altitude bakers, I have adjusted the recipe for the Seven-Minute Frosting to produce better results. I've reduced the amount of water slightly, but even so, the frosting will take longer to beat and will not be quite as fluffy as that produced at lower altitudes. It still looks gorgeous on Red Velvet and dark chocolate cakes, as evidenced by the photo on a previous page, which was taken in the mountains. The frosting will hold up for two days when the cake is chilled, after which it transforms into a sticky marshmallow texture that is difficult to slice. YIELDS FROSTING FOR A 2-LAYER CAKE

INGREDIENTS

2	egg whites, at room temperature
¼	cup water
¼	teaspoon cream of tartar
1¼	cups granulated sugar
½	teaspoon vanilla

Bring a saucepan of water to a simmer. Place egg whites and ¼ cup water in a heat-proof bowl and beat with an electric mixer until the mixture begins to foam. Add cream of tartar and beat 1 minute until the egg whites start to thicken. Place the bowl over simmering water, but do not allow the bowl to touch the water. Continue beating until the egg whites double in volume.

Gradually add sugar, beating until the frosting is thick and glossy, about 15 to 20 minutes. Remove it from the heat and stir in the vanilla. Frost the cake and chill until ready to serve.

Pavlova with Raspberry Sorbet and Strawberries

Individual meringue Pavlovas, filled with raspberry sorbet and juicy, sweet strawberries, make a stunning dessert any time of the year, and especially for special occasions. Fluffy meringue is spooned into a cake decorating bag and piped onto parchment-covered cookie sheets in swirls shaped like miniature bird's nests, then baked in a slow oven for 1½ hours until firm. I prefer to leave the meringues in the oven overnight to be sure they dry completely, which prevents them from becoming sticky.

Both Australia and New Zealand claim to have invented the Pavlova, possibly in tribute to Russian prima ballerina Anna Pavlova, who toured both countries in 1926 and was described as floating through the air when dancing. This light, airy meringue dessert can be a fitting grand finale to any memorable celebration, and is certain to garner a standing ovation. YIELDS 8 SERVINGS

INGREDIENTS

3	egg whites, at room temperature
¼	teaspoon cream of tartar
6	tablespoons sugar
½	teaspoon vanilla
1	pint fresh strawberries, rinsed and hulled
2	tablespoons sugar
1	14-ounce container raspberry sorbet

Preheat the oven to 225 degrees. In the large bowl of an electric mixer, whip egg whites on high speed until they are foamy, add cream of tartar, and continue whipping. Gradually add sugar, whip until soft peaks form, and add the vanilla. Continue whipping until the meringue is glossy and forms stiff peaks.

Transfer the meringue to a large piping bag fitted with an Ateco 867 or other star tip. Add several dabs of meringue to the corners of a baking sheet and cover it with parchment paper. Starting with the center, pipe a 3-inch wide circle of meringue onto the parchment paper to form two layers. Bake 1½ hours, then turn off the heat and allow the meringues to dry in the oven several hours or overnight.

Slice the strawberries, place them in a bowl, and sprinkle them with sugar. Stir gently, cover, and chill. To serve, fill each Pavolova with a small scoop of raspberry sorbet and garnish with fresh strawberries.

INDEX